AS THE SUN CLIMBS

SMALL BOYS WITH GREAT ENTHUSIASM
(On the top of our hill)

AS THE SUN CLIMBS

by

RITA F. SNOWDEN

'I have seen these things in a shaft of
sunlight.'
—T. S. ELIOT

LONDON: THE EPWORTH PRESS

Published by
THE EPWORTH PRESS
(FRANK H. CUMBERS)
25—35 City Road, London, E.C.1.

*

New York . Toronto
Melbourne . Cape Town

PRINTED IN GREAT BRITAIN BY
EBENEZER BAYLIS AND SON, LTD., THE
TRINITY PRESS, WORCESTER, AND LONDON

Dedicated
to my Parents—
country people,
and dear

ACKNOWLEDGMENTS

I would like to express my warm thanks to the following Authors and their Publishers for permission to quote from their works.

THE Executors of the late John Drinkwater and Messrs. Sidgwick & Jackson, Ltd., for 'And lies bore lies' and 'What more of life than this' from *Collected Poems*; the Executors of the late W. J. Turner and Messrs. Sidgwick & Jackson, Ltd., for 'And the Winds Came' from *Ecstasy*; the Executors of the late E. V. Lucas and Messrs. Methuen & Co. Ltd., for lines from *Writing and Remembering*; Mr. J. Middleton Murry and the Society of Authors for the quotation 'The more I see of life' by Katherine Mansfield. Miss Vera Brittain and Messrs. Macmillan & Co. Ltd., for lines from *Testament of Friendship*; Mr. Allan B. Crawford and Messrs. Hodder & Stoughton Ltd., for lines from *I Went to Tristan*; the Executors of the late Earl Baldwin and Messrs. Hodder & Stoughton for an extract from *On England*; Sir John Simon and Messrs. Hodder & Stoughton for a quotation from *Portrait of my Mother* and James S. Stewart and Messrs. Hodder & Stoughton Ltd. for the lines from *The Heralds of God*; Miss V. Sackville-West and Messrs. William Heinemann Ltd., for a quotation from *The Land*. The Executors of the late Edward Thomas and Messrs. J. M. Dent & Sons Ltd., for a quotation from *South Country*, and Mr. Fred Kitchen and Messrs. J. M. Dent & Sons Ltd., for the lines from *Songs of Sherwood*. Miss Grace Noll Crowell and Messrs. Pearn, Pollinger & Higham Ltd., for a quotation from *Songs of Hope*; the Trustees of the Mary Webb Estate and

Messrs. Jonathan Cape Ltd. for some lines from *Poems and the Spring of Joy*; the Executors of the late C. E. Montague and Messrs. Chatto & Windus for an extract from *Action*. The Executrix of the late Major the Hon. Maurice Baring and Messrs. William Heinemann Ltd. for some lines from *Round the World in Any Number of Days*; the Executors of the late Edward Thomas and the Falcon Press for two extracts from *The Prose of Edward Thomas*; Mr. Lewis Wilshire and the Editor of the *British Weekly* for the poem 'The beauty of their faith'; and Mr. Augustus Muir and Messrs. Methuen & Co. Ltd. for quotations from *Heather Track and High Road*. Mr. Alan Ross and Messrs. John Lehmann Ltd. for 'Some things can be logged' from *Time Was Away*; Miss E. Arnot Robertson and Messrs. George Allen & Unwin Ltd., for a quotation from *What is a Book?* and the Executrix of the late Alistair MacLean and the Moray Press for the quotations on pages 239 and 240. The Executrix of the late G. K. Chesterton and Messrs. Sheed & Ward for a quotation from *G. K. Chesterton* by Maisie Ward; Mr. Ernest Raymond and Messrs. Cassell & Co. Ltd. for the quotation from *Through Literature to Life*; and finally, I should like to thank my doctor for his kindness in checking certain facts contained in Chapter XII.

R.F.S.

ILLUSTRATIONS

FOREWORD

'*What would you like for your birthday?*' I looked up. What would I like? My friend was going into the town.

When she returned, I called: 'I have thought of something for my birthday.' And a few hours later, I had my present—a sunrise together.

We rose at four. The air was crisp; we got into woollen sweaters. My friend made the beds; I made a pot of tea. Then stealthily we crept from the house.

The world was still. We reached the Hill at a swinging step. Morning was just breaking. Sheep were stretching wakefully. The Waitemata harbour lay etched in silver where it ran in a narrow strip out-reaching to the Manukau.

A little wind was stirring in the old pine at the top of the Hill. We walked round it, turned up our coat collars—it was fresh—found a sheltered spot, and waited.

What would it be like? Would there be cloud?

A gash at the horizon revealed a warm reddy-chrome. Gradually it stretched its loveliness out along the coast. Yes, it was going to be perfect.

A solitary lark rose from the grass at our feet, and hanging above our heads, trilled and trilled. And presently, his *matins* done, he dropped as suddenly to earth.

The sun was above the horizon now. It was coming up with a splendour of gold. To the right the transformed mud-flats of the Manukau were opalescent. To the left were pale pink fluffy clouds like the playthings of cherubim. The glory was of the land now. The sun increased. The blue hills, layer upon layer, as far as the eye could see, took on a more substantial look. The houses began to show

9

up on the western ranges. Turning, we picked out the headlands far round the coast, beyond the sleeping city.

The colour strengthened. The trees, clumped comfortably at the foot of the Hill, changed as we looked. And still we stood.

The new day had come—for me a rather special day—my fortieth birthday!

As the morning advanced, 'Postie' brought me my birthday-mail—and a letter from a stranger. She wrote: 'I have just finished your book, *A Thousand Sunrises*, and could wish there were a thousand more.'

As I re-read her letter, I found myself thinking: But there are more—thirteen-thousand-six-hundred more—and some of them significant.

If my unknown friend ever comes upon this book, I hope she will like it. I will not call it autobiography—but to start with a sunrise and a birthday is a start as interesting as any other. There must be some essential link between my fortieth and my first.

Many of us, like E. V. Lucas, feel that to write an autobiography before three-score-years-and-ten is slightly indelicate. E. V. L. got over his difficulty very neatly by going to bed for five weeks with lumbago. He said it made him feel years older, so he filled in the time writing his autobiography. His excuse is no better than my own. I have a good crisp memory now, but I cannot say what it will be like at seventy.

To absolve myself from the presumption of the unimportant, I ought to say that my real reason for writing this book is that I shall have a good time doing so. I have put in some pictures. It is usual in a book of this sort to rummage out pictures of the author at various stages—before her baby curls were cut, when she played hockey for her boarding-school. But I never had any baby curls, or a boarding-school. So I have simplified the custom and have chosen instead some pictures of things I have loved—all pictures I have made myself.

An ever-present danger, of course, is that one should impute to childhood and youth, experiences and ideas which came but yesterday. I will try not to cheat.

I can promise but little to those whose chief interest is in the dredging of the subconscious. I still believe in the precious rights of privacy. Suffice to say briefly: I am single, having come several times to the cross-roads of choice; I am grateful for life—it has never seemed to me so good; I have found my vocation—I get paid for doing what, given the bare chance, I would do for nothing.

But the sun is already up. . . .

I

I CANNOT remember my first sunrise. That's a pity. I cannot remember my first birthday, or my first discovery of hands and feet, my first song, or book, or my first entrancing peep of skies and fields.

My first clear memory is of a bit of adventuring I did on my own account. Somehow I lost my chubby balance, and came up on my back, beetle-like, under the old kitchen-table. I have a distinct remembrance of that strange wooden thing over my head. That was my first surprise in a world full of surprises. I ought now to suffer from some kind of phobia, according to the psychologists—*claustrophobia*, I think it is—but I don't. Some people will persist in turning life into 'a case'.

I ought, however, for the sake of truth, and my sister, to speak of 'our birthdays', and 'our lives'—because I'm a twin. But from the start, we were rather odd twins.

In his learned *Inquiries into Human Faculty* Dr. Francis Galton devotes a hundred or more pages to the history of twins. 'Their history', he says, 'affords means of distinguishing between the effects of tendencies received at birth, and of those that were imposed by the special circumstances of their after-lives'—in other words, the effects of heredity and environment. 'Extreme similarity between twins of the same sex', he says, 'is nearly as common as moderate resemblance.'

Ours, from the start, was a case of 'extreme dissimilarity'—from the time that we could choose, my sister dressed her dollies and kept house, whilst I roamed the fields and read books. She lives now in the South Island, a happily married woman with her family, whilst I live in the North, a single woman with a happiness of another

13

sort—though perhaps we are nearer to each other now than we've ever been.

I still tease her about how she got her 'red hair'—in reality, hair brown in some lights, golden in others. And she doesn't like my teasing any more than she ever did. Happily, the South Island is rather a long way from the North, and she can't throw things at me now.

The tale of how she got her 'red hair' is a family joke, and like most family jokes, has improved with the telling.

One night, when our father was away from the farm, our mother conceived the idea of milking the house-cow. Accordingly, she lashed the leg of the cow to the paling-fence by the kitchen-window, and sat down to milk. Her head into Strawberry's glossy flank, the warm needle of milk hissed into the pail. At first it sang against the hollow tin base. As the moments passed, it murmured with a frothy satisfaction.

Off and on, she popped up to see how her twins were getting on. She could see their every movement through the kitchen-window—or thought she could. Only when she came indoors, her task done, did she discover that one of them had climbed on to the kitchen-table, and had eaten all the heads off the box of matches lying in the candle-stick.

Wax-matches! Poisonous wax-matches! For a minute she was at a loss to know what to do. Then with country presence of mind, she remembered the little bottle in the medicine-cupboard.

Darkness came, and when she could bear the suspense no longer, she bundled up her babies in their shawls, and started off along the road to meet their father.

She met him down by the blue-gums.

The young couple returned, lit the lamp, put the babies down, and sat up till midnight.

And nothing happened! The naughty twin wasn't even

14

sick. And only the family-joke remains now to say that for ever afterwards she was blessed with 'red hair and a fiery temper'.

We were born in Hope, in the wide pastoral district of Nelson. Nelson is one of the nicest places in which to be born. Everywhere there are trees—English trees, spiring poplars, oaks, willows, elms, backing the snug little town, and bordering its wide farming plains—changing from hour to hour; green in spring, parchment in high summer. And always there are hills; and beyond them ranges—blue ranges, and far beyond them, mighty peaks, snowcapped in winter. The district is set upon a bay whose blue waters break rhythmically upon a curve of exquisite sand.

Nelson gets more sunshine than any other part of the country—more, indeed, than the south of Italy. So good, simple things follow each other in quick profusion.

Its soil is like the Garden of Eden. It grows apples so abundantly that they create their own problems.

The district is made up of small farms and orchards. Nobody has much land; nobody has much wealth. If the orchards fail, the corn will be good; if the corn fails, the cows will not fail. Over all broods a mood snug and secure—one of the most important things in the world to a child.

By the time one comes to nineteen, it may be time to move away to where there are more hazards, but till then, Nelson, snug and secure, graced with running streams and girdled with blue mountains, is a lovely place in which to grow up.

A child has the chance to know pretty thoroughly the piece of country into which she is born. She lives her early years very near the earth. She knows the smell of the soil, bees bobbing over the clover, the smell of peppermint by the stream, the shape of weeds and grasses, the magic of

15

clouds piled high. Every day is like the first day of creation.

My up-growing years were filled with the dear delights of earth. The world was big then. In the summer we lay in the long grass, and told each other's fortunes—'Tinker, tailor, soldier, sailor . . .' If by unhappy chance a fortune didn't come out right, we gaily nipped off a bit at the end, and never worried—a fortune could be changed at will, we thought.

We had our little worries and concerns. We were frightened of the dark, of a chimney on fire, and of God.

We knew what we meant to be when we grew up, though we changed it over and over again before the time came.

Three times a year we went to town—a considerable journey, that has shrunk to a paltry thirteen miles. Returning, half-asleep and wholly content, the slow, heavy clopping of the horse's hoofs in our ears, peace was in it, if not speed.

There were excursions of the mind, too. As we sat high in an old tree, or lay under a hawthorn minding the cows on the roadside, we knew we should evermore live in a world of wide distances.

The seasons moved from month to month like a back-cloth to the characters. The plough was guided down the sweet furrows, the gulls from the sea six miles off following after. The seed was sown, the harvest awaited, the hedges clipped. Much water has run under the old bridge, and growth been clipped from the hedges, since I sighted my first nestful of young birds, their gaping yellow beaks opened widely to a beneficent world.

We had no near neighbours. For weeks we saw no outsiders, save the butcher, baker and grocer, and perhaps, the men from the Mill—a lovely old flax-mill built by the Rutherford family. It had a transparent mill-stream with

trout in it, and a wooden water-wheel. No single sound of
Nature was like the sound of that water-wheel on a
summer's day. It remains a wonder to me that the four
men who had most to do with it could become so used to it
that it did not make them drowsy. Perhaps it did.

We lived in 'Clover Road', though it was a long time
before we knew that it had a name. It was just 'our road'.
It meandered down from the hills beyond which each new
day came to us, and lost itself in short grass at the river-
side, and the road to the Mill. Now and again a 'swagger'
came down it, with a hunger and thirst, otherwise we
knew all who travelled up and down, and what business
they had. They would greet us as they passed: ' 'Lo,
Children!' ''Lo, George!'

Part of our farm was in white clover. And countless
bee-stings I got as I crossed by the tiny meadow-path
with my father's lunch, or skipped bare-footed down the
lane to bring up the cows. Hours and hours I spent watching the bees at their in-gathering, or upon my knees looking for a lucky four-leaved clover. All purpose then was in
an hour, all summer in a flower.

> *And the winds came and purified my limbs,*
> *And the stars came and set within my eyes,*
> *And sunny clouds rested upon my shoulders,*
> *And the blue sky shimmered deep within me,*
> *And I sang like a carven pipe of music!*

Added to the delights of bees and fields were those of
orchard and garden. I will speak but little of the garden—
it had its restrictions, like Eden. Our mother stood over it
as with a flaming sword, in the fruiting season, with a view
to preserves and jams. We children always discovered the
first gooseberries that were ripe. There was the little
transparent kind, early—and if we could leave them alone
long enough—sweet. Later came the big fat veined ones,

and their delicious insides popped out rudely as we bit into them.

And I will speak but little of the orchard. Plums came first after the blossoming, followed quickly by apricots, peaches and pears.

I can never expect to be happier than in those early mornings, when my ears were blessed with the hiss of the scythe through the grass, and the whirr of the hone sharpening the blade. Morning after morning, then a thrush sang from a favourite tree-top:

> *Get up, get!*
> *Be quick, be quick, be quick!*
> *Stick to it, stick to it!*

We had no church nearer than the village—the picturesque old Anglican church in which we had been christened. We were taken there on that occasion in two halves of a hamper in the back of the trap; and from what I have been told, showed a little unwillingness to receive our names.

When we could attend church again, a few peppermints were needed to keep us quiet in sermon-time. When these gave out, a surreptitious game of trains could be indulged in by silently pushing prayer-books along the book-rack.

It was always difficult for our parents to get to church. We kept no help. When our brother arrived, the difficulty increased, though we had help for a time. There were many things to be done on a one-man farm on a Sunday morning.

We heard talk of Sunday-school, but the river, with its two bridges, stood in the way of that plan. We might have crossed safely, could we have gone alone, but the Palmer children, whom we should meet in with a mile upon our way, went over the railway-bridge—constructed of 'sleepers', with wide gaps—and our parents were not keen.

So when a little Methodist Sunday-school was opened, about the same distance in the other direction, our father, with some relief, harnessed old Jack, and took us there.

It was a simple Sunday-school, run by two young fruit-growers, the Bateup brothers. The first morning, in good time, we set off with our father in the trap, wearing our spotless embroidered frocks, our faces shining with innocence and soap.

But we had hardly got to the top of Burke's Bank, when old Jack shied, and all but threw us out. Sitting alongside my father, my feet dangling in space, I fell, and seemed likely to go over the step, when my father made a grab at me. As he did so, a strained handful of hooks and eyes and the back of my dress came away in his hand.

Man-like, it never occurred to him to go back—we were going to Sunday-school, and to Sunday-school we went. When we got there he explained to the big girls what had happened—*and they fixed me up with pins*.

That was my first meeting with the Methodist Church that I have loved and served, wept over and marvelled at ever since!

Year by year, when summer was fully come, great billies of tea went to the brown-armed men in the fields, sweltering under the sun. Sober neighbours came in to help. The tall 'Sigglekow boys' brought along mouth-organs and pitch-forks, and in between work taught us children to sing 'Pretty Red-Wing'. Under the grateful shade of the stack, we loved our lunch-times together. Against the neighbouring farmers, these lounging, laughing boys seemed like giants and minstrels from another world.

Always at the end of summer, the engine and thresher came—pulling into our yard the night before the work was to be done. It was with difficulty that we stayed at the table long enough to eat our porridge the next morning. Things were happening in the stack-yard.

The engine and thresher belonged to that world of wonder between the accepted death of story-book dragons, and the birth of this new age of machine-dragons.

By the time we had squeezed through the opening in the fence, the engine would be merry with smoke and steam. Its fly-wheel turned with the importance of the universe. The little cluster of bells that our father called 'the governor', halfway along the body of the monster, winked in the sunshine. A great belt swung between the engine and the thresher.

Two men, forks in hand, balanced themselves on the stack. They looked like young gods against the sky, though by the afternoon we knew that they would be brought down from their exalted position.

A third man guided the sheaves into the thresher's innards, and at the end of its long elevator where distracted straw came out of its yammering body, two others stood, building a stack—oblong—but without the prestige of the first. It was only straw.

The most important man in our eyes was the strong young farmer who hooked on the bags, and in an amazingly short time received them again full of corn. As we watched, wondering what would happen if he forgot to hook on a new bag, he deftly shut off the supply, and swung the full bag on to noisy iron scales near by. Then with a speed that astonished, he threaded his gleaming curved needle and sewed up the bags.

When all the strange men, the thresher, the engine, and the 'Sigglekow boys' had gone, only the full bags and the straw-stack remained.

The big straw-stack was slippery at first, and it smelled nice. By degrees its freshness went, and it settled down.

And by degrees the cows and calves burrowed into it, and we children played magic caves about it.

Long summer evenings were our times for such fun. The dews fell, the big moths came out, and the moon rose over the far hills. We raced ourselves breathlessly happy, until from a window showing soft lamplight, our mother called, and drunk with weariness, we dragged ourselves in, took off our boots, and washed and slept.

II

WE were sent to school the day our brother was born. We were seven. Hitherto, one thing had happened at a time; now two exciting things happened at once. Our parents—poor innocents—knew no psychology; I doubt whether they had even happened on the term. So it never occurred to them to prepare us for the first event, as they prepared us for the second.

I remember still our father's patience night after night, after he'd taken off his boots. A timeless picture we made, the firelight blessing us. Patiently he persisted: 'Five, six, seven, eight, nine.'' But try as I would, I couldn't get up higher than seven. My sister raced me: 'Seven-eight-nine-ten.'

Then a night or two before we were due for school, I achieved it. It was late-shopping night in the village, a couple of miles off, and our father was due there some-time before closing hour, to buy at our mother's direction a piece of kitchen curtain. His patience, perhaps, was a little less spacious that night. 'Five-six-seven': I stopped. 'When are you going to buy the curtain?' Again he tried: 'Five-six-seven-eight. Will we still be up when you come back?'

Our mother had somehow endowed that strong, plain piece of curtain with a fairy-like transparency. Perhaps it was because it was to come from Mrs. Fairey's shop—an efficient, somewhat crowded extension of the village Post Office.

The little country school—divided unceremoniously in-to 'Infants' and 'Big Room'—was several miles off in the

LONG JOURNEYS WITH A LOAD OF BOOKS
(My van and caravan)

A PEACEFUL GREEN PLACE
(Near home)

opposite direction. It stood under great trees which roared with a strange energy when the wind was high.

We loved all that went on in that little kingdom of learning, once we got over our introduction.

That first morning our father took us down in the trap. The Headmaster came out. They talked together in serious tones. Then we were delicately and firmly removed to the Infant Room.

We sat side by side, under the eye of the Infants Mistress—a kindly woman with a soft voice, and a little tin of soda in her cupboard for children who got toothache.

Our arrival, a good hour after school had begun, must have upset her morning's work. After we had shown the entire room our new school-bags, and what we had for lunch, we surrendered ourselves to mild discipline, and were set to do pot-hooks; but soon this particular educational sport failed to interest us.

The second day, Nurse Palmer who had mysteriously arrived in our home and established herself, sent us down, perched high on the butcher's cart. The butcher had several calls to make before we could reach school. At each gate, a farmer's wife came out, tucking up her apron, large white plate in hand. When the butcher told where we were going, each made some odd adult remark about our 'liking school'. We kept our thoughts to ourselves.

Again, we were set to do pot-hooks—*but we had already done them*.

By lunch-time, that second day, we were home. We'd had enough of school!

William Canton's words have a strange beauty: 'The great globe swings round out of the dark into the sun; there is always morning somewhere; and for ever in this shifting region, the morning-light sees the little ones afoot——

'He sees them in country lanes and rustic villages; on lonely moorlands . . . on the hillsides . . . in the woods, on the stepping-stones that cross the brook in the glen; along the sea-cliffs, and on the water-ribbed sands; trespassing on the railway lines; making short-cuts through the corn; in the crowded streets of smoky cities; in small rocky islands; in places far inland where the sea is known only as a strange tradition.

'And as new nations with *their* cities and villages, their fields, woods, mountains and sea-shores rise up into the morning-side, lo! fresh troops, and still fresh troops, and yet again fresh troops of these school-going children of the dawn!'

In time we got started again. Pot-hooks led on to lesson-books, and lesson-books to other things. Soon, nothing short of tooth-ache, mumps, or a flooded creek could keep us at home.

Once or twice every winter the creek was expected to flood. The water ran over the road at 'the willows'—a hollow in our road—and at 'Palmer's Corner'. Sometimes the deluge would be short-lived—though we had stayed from school—the sky would break blue, and the sun would come out. Then we went to paddle, where the water ran shallow over the roadway giggling in the sunlight.

Sometimes the storm lasted for nights and days, and the river flooded. That was more serious. But we loved those days, and the moment especially, when his wet-weather work finished, our father strolled down to the kitchen to make us a pot of toffee. I think he welcomed those times as much as we did. Our mother never showed enthusiasm —I think she was a little anxious for her pots. We thought it wonderful that a father could make toffee. We accepted it as natural that he could make other things—whistles when the willows were out, pop-guns from elderberry-sticks and a piece of corset steel, bubble-pipes from bamboo, cricket-bats, and swing-seats.

Our mother made things, too—clothes, garden-beds, and good golden crusty bread. But somehow, the things that she made never quickened my imagination like those my father made. I wanted to make things like my father made. I wanted to have a pocket-knife. Pocket-knives were wonderful things.

Many and many an hour I spent in the springtime before the sappy wood had hardened, wondering solemnly what I would make out of a willow stick, or a knotty piece from the wood-heap. I think my pocket-knife did more for my imagination, than anything else I can think of. Years later, I was ready to take instant delight in G. K. Chesterton, when I met him recording his possessions at a certain stage of his up-growing. He listed with joy: 'An unwieldy sort of pocket-knife.' In addition to its blades, it had a thing for getting stones out of a horse's hoofs. 'What a beautiful sense of security it gives one', said he, 'to reflect that if one should ever have money enough to buy a horse, and should happen to buy one, and the horse should happen to have a stone in his hoof—that one is ready; one stands prepared with a defiant smile!'

I preserved complete and unquestioning a belief in my father's omniscience and omnipotence, until one day I came upon him using his pocket-knife, and begged him to make '*a set of doll's teeth*' from a piece of knotted fire wood. I can still feel the jolt of that moment, when he had to confess that my request was beyond him. I had never dreamed that anything was beyond my father—and his pocket-knife.

Happily, he had powers of another kind. He knew the calls of birds, and likely nesting-places. He taught me where to look for wild violets, and for the little green-backed beetles that ran up the grass stalks. He taught me to eat sorrel—the leaves that were not too bitter. He taught me to gather hips and haws, and to tell the names of the grasses. He led my imagination out into a wide and wonderful world.

When tomatoes first came, he and I were the only ones in our family to eat them. I disliked them intensely, but I wouldn't have failed my father. When the Chinese green-grocer who gardened a neighbour's land sent us a caddy of China tea, it was my father and I who drank it, though Christmas had caught up on us again before we got to the bottom of the caddy.

We knew little of shops. Mrs. Tebay kept one at the Post Office at Hope, three miles off. And there was Mrs. Fairey's shop, and one or two others in the village, half-an-hour off in the other direction. Our only ice-cream was to be had from a saucer of milk up on a post-top—out of the way of the cat—on a winter's night. In the morning it yielded little milky crystals.

If we got round to buying a bar of honey-comb toffee, one or other of us begged to be allowed to slide a penny out of a carefully-guarded money-box with a kitchen-knife. Next morning we took it to school. Then the penny changed hands—the Tebay children took it home, and gave it to their mother. If they didn't forget, they brought the toffee to school the next morning. But they were the most famous family in the school for lateness, and one could not tell until playtime whether they had brought it or not: so easily they forgot an important thing like a penny bar of toffee. Then there was nothing to do but to start all over again. It always seemed to me that the cost of that toffee was too high. I can feel the aches of disappointment now.

Except for these simple transactions, I had seldom a penny in my pocket until I was ten.

Then out of consideration for our farmers and fruit-growers, the County Council announced that it was willing to pay three-pence per dozen for birds' eggs—thrushes' and blackbirds'. Starlings and sparrows nested high, and came later. For them it was prepared to pay 'fourpence per dozen'. And a footnote stated plainly that the Council was prepared to pay 'sixpence per dozen for birds' heads and legs'. Rarer birds were protected.

So a fruitful field of finance was opened in the spring. I cannot remember that it had any unhappy effects upon my love for birds; certainly it had a good effect upon my observation, and it broadened my familiarity with the countryside.

'Blackies'—blackbirds—came first. Their nests were low down, large and clumsy, with small sitting-space lined with mud. 'Thrushies'—thrushes—came next. They built in thick gorse and hawthorn hedges. Their nests were lighter—they used a lot of soft rotted wood. And they laid three lovely bluey eggs, with spots.

Those of us who 'did bird-nesting', had a sort of understanding about our beats. I took in, of right, all the hedges on our farm, and several beyond it. A piece of the river-bed was mine, too. This proved the most fascinating part of my little world to date. I got to know every gorse bush and willow-tree there, much better than I knew my near relations.

Saturdays were glorious days when I went off early with my treacle tin, my lunch and a stick; days of billowing clouds, and deep smells—golden heavy-scented gorse, broom, willows! Occasionally, beside the Mill-stream, I crushed peppermint or penny-royal.

Human senses, I have learned since, are poor things compared with the senses of many of God's creatures. At our best, we cannot smell like a dog, or migrate like a bird. But in childhood, our senses are not spoiled by highly-

seasoned food, or food itself, by talk of calories and vita-
mins.

By sundown, when I must bring home the cows, I would
have my treacle-tin half full of eggs, my clothes full of
holes, and my heart full of content.

My sister seemed scarcely to take account of these
delights. I realize now that she did the things that most
little girls did—nice little girls. She dressed and undressed
her dollies, and mother taught her to cook. I realize now
that she was fortunate, for mother was justly famed for her
cooking. But I managed, somehow, to keep off the
'Beeton' track.

Of course, when the seasons drew in, I spent more of my
energies indoors. Books were my first love—reading-
books, drawing-books. I suppose there must have been a
time when I did not have a pencil and book in my hand—
but I do not remember it. I fancy I began by chewing the
corners of rag books.

We hadn't very many books, till we children started
bringing home prizes from school. Thirty or forty staid
volumes stood side by side in the varnished book-case with
glass doors. My father had besides half-a-dozen of his
own—treasured, not for what they said, but because they
were the work of his grandfather, John Snowden—written
in his marvellous copper-plate hand. I still think them the
loveliest books I have ever seen. Now that I have them in
my keeping, I turn to them often. I know nothing of any
other Snowden with a passion for books; but my father's
reverence for his grandfather, and admiration for his
beautiful writing, raised the craft of letters high in my
childish imagination.

My only regret is that I do not know more about
'scholar John', who inscribed them so long ago. He lived
a little way out of York, and every Sunday, according to
family tradition, walked into York, to worship in the

Minster, and to take down in a system of shorthand he had devised, the sermon that he heard.

My mind drifted, not unnaturally, one day, as I sat silent in the Minster, just after I had published a book of my own with an English publisher.

Somehow, my sister managed without my passion for books. But I had so many questions—questions I did not even know how to ask. Somewhere, I felt there must surely be an answer. I could not know that at that moment, the beloved Q, lecturer at Cambridge, was saying: 'The master-key admitting a child to all, or almost all palaces of knowledge is his ability *to read*. When he has grasped the key of his mother-tongue he can with perseverance, unlock all doors to all avenues of knowledge. More—he has the passport to heavens unguessed.'

Again and again as my love of books grew, my father brought me a parcel of an entrancing oblong shape— still my favourite shape for a parcel. They came pretty regularly at Christmasses and birthdays, and he brought me home occasionally pieces of poetry that he had found.

Unless it was a matter of mumps, measles, or minding the cows on the roadside, I was forbidden to read in the daytime. Daytimes were for work, night-times for books, when the lamp was lit. But the hours beneath the soft glow were never long enough. Before I could discover where 'Deerfoot' would reappear in the forest, or 'The Little Women' get out of their troubles, my father or mother would be bound to glance up at the old clock on the mantelshelf. How I hated its voice: 'Tick! tack! tick! tack!'

Sometimes, in the daytime, I stuck a book up my blouse, and read when I should have been doing something else, weeding, or pumping the water for the cows. My parents were anxious that I should not over-strain my

29

eyes. Print then was often unreasonably small, as though printers and opticians were in some nefarious alliance.

At the ambitious age of eleven I founded, edited and illustrated a magazine. It was printed in blue pencil. Sometimes my readers sent me contributions—or more correctly, my *listeners*, for there was only ever one copy, and it was never allowed out of the editor's hands. All those who wanted to know what was in it, had to have it read aloud to them. Copies of this illustrious journal hung for years on my editorial nail in the apple-room, at the head of the stairs. It was my first serious literary work—*and it was very serious!*

III

THERE was always in childhood the dread possibility that the chimney might catch on fire. It had happened once. First came the smell that something in our safe little world was burning, then the fact that it was the chimney, then visible from the outside the flames leaping up. Our mother quickly opened the front of the range and put on a shovelful of sulphur. That made the flames a funny colour. And my sister and I ran into the house-paddock by the wood-heap. Presently, our father climbed a ladder propped against the chimney, and put a wet sack on its top.

Next to the chimney catching fire, and the extraordinary bravery of our father, the thing that scared me most was a fierce gander we had that flapped its great wings and hissed. When it attacked little brother, our mother threw a piece of firewood at it, and disabled it.

Pig-killing I hated, too. The washing-copper was moved from its accustomed place that day, and put on to boil up by the pig-sty. While the actual killing was going on, we children were sent to the neighbours, but before we could get away the animal's squealing filled the whole farm. With our hands clapped over our ears, we ran on, but no hands could clap out that sound.

When the hot blood had gushed to the ground, the carcase was stretched on a trestle, and the two strange men who had done the deed, joined our father in scraping the scalded hide.

In a few minutes, our mother would come upon the scene with her big oval meat-dish. Pig-trotters, 'spare-ribs', and 'scraps' then became our succulent joy for days.

The trotters, which we children liked best, consisted of sinewy, sweet gristle.

The bladder, well cleaned, was used for storing lard. Some people made sausages, but we never did. Sausages were much favoured among our German friends at the little village of Ranzau, a few miles off. Every year, our father and mother went down to help the Schwass's with their pig-killing.

While the early, unpleasant part was going on, the daughter of the house—who loved bright beads, and wore her hair in the German fashion—led us children off to the little store to look in at the window, where always it seemed, a fly buzzed about. After a time, having parted with our penny, we each drew a bull's eye from our tiny bag, and walked homewards swollen-cheeked.

At mid-day the men were called in to a great meal, and pig-killing became something of a festival.

When the meal was cleared away, we children spent the afternoon getting in the way. The women-folk, with great aprons about them, and sleeves rolled, settled into an orgy of sausage-making. It lasted two days, sometimes a third, but we had our horse and trap, and came home at night.

Mrs. Schwass could not have lived happily through a pig-killing without her black puddings. Neither our father nor mother cared for these delicacies, so we children never tasted them.

What we liked best was to see the big brown hams and sides of bacon hanging up under the rafters of our own dairy.

In springtime there were other interests—lambs came early into Palmer's paddock, just across the way. They stood, at first, on wobbly legs, their complacent mothers nibbling with quivering nostrils. And there were young things on our own farm. Morning by morning we might hear the feeble complaint of young calves. When they were taken from their mothers, we children tried to teach them to drink, allowing them to suck our fingers in a bucket of warm, white, foamy milk.

And there were hen's eggs to be hunted. The hens were provided with nesting-boxes, but they much preferred the gorse hedges. Our mother spoke of their 'laying-away' as a bother, but we children rejoiced in it. Sometimes an old hen would evade us so long that before we could match our cunning with hers, she would have a nest of fifteen or sixteen eggs. Sometimes we would miss her altogether until one morning she would come walking toward us with a little family of yellow chicks.

We kept ducks, too. They also 'laid away'. To collect their eggs was always an adventure. They trailed off, in a long line behind each other in the morning, after they had eaten their mash, and layed in Biggar's Pond. Biggar's Pond was out of bounds for us, save when our mother allowed us to go with her, carrying between us the longest-handled hoe we possessed. With this she raked out the duck-eggs that were rightly her property.

Mushrooms were another seasonable joy. The best place for them was Palmer's paddock. They were to be spied there in great semi-circles—tiny button-like ones, and big ones, all pinkly pleated underneath. There was an element of surprise in creeping out in the early morning, the grass still pearled, the posts of the fence casting long, slender shadows. We neither knew nor cared that an ancient book had recorded: 'Many do fear the goodly mushrooms as poysonous, damp weeds; but this does in no ways abate the exceeding excellence of God's Providance that out of the grass and dew where nothing was, and where onlie the little worm turned in his sporte, come, as at the shaking of bells, these delicate meates.'

These joys were the greater for being seasonal joys, as were the games we played. They had their peculiar and

unaccountable seasons, as children's games always have.
For weeks, marbles would be the thing: then they would
as suddenly disappear, but while they lasted, we gave our
eager hearts to them. The boys carried little print bags
each tied with a grubby tape, and pulled them from their
pockets like proud merchants showing off their pearls.
The girls treasured theirs a little more openly. Some of
the marbles were beautiful—'glassies' had within them
little spiral threads of many colours. Many and many an
hour I puzzled how they got their colours inside. Clear
'glassies' could be broken from ginger-beer bottles, though
it was risky. One might lose an eye in getting a marble.
'Stonies' could be bought at five-a-penny. I carried two
beautiful 'glassies' that had belonged to my father. Certainly they were chipped, but that only made them the
more valuable in my eyes; that showed the battles they
had fought.

There were also 'alleys', and best of all, 'blood-alleys',
cut from alabaster. The red vein in them was real blood,
the boys said. Only a few owned such super-marbles. We
played variations of the game: 'pyramids', 'stand-up
megs', and 'ring-taw'. Ring-taw was easily the favourite.
Someone, with a strong finger or a stick, drew a ring
on the hard dust-swept ground. Therein we placed our
marbles, two from each player. Six feet away another
ring was drawn, and the play began. The beginner knelt,
his hand against the outer line, his 'taw' between the
knuckle of his bent thumb and the curve of his forefinger.
Suddenly, he straightened his thumb. There were rules,
of course, as strict as the 'Laws of Moses'. Pains attendant
on dirty knees scrubbed hard at bedtime, and stubbed
toes, we accepted. Sometimes one went home with a
greatly increased bag.

Then as suddenly, and unaccountably, tops would be
all the rage. We made our own. There was a knack in it.

A well-spun top made a hum like a contented bee, lovely to youthful ears.

The ancient art of top-spinning reaches back earlier than the fourteenth century, when children played at whipping tops. Little pictures of them appear in the margins of books of that time. Sir Thomas More 'set the top', in the spacious days before he got caught up in the affairs of State. He wrote:

> *I am called Childhood, to play is all my mind,*
> *To cast a kyte, a cokstele and a ball,*
> *A top can I set, and drive it in its kind.*

And with boy-like spirit, he added:

> *And would to God these hateful bookes*
> *All were in a fire burnt to powder.*

Shakespeare put words about his top on to Falstaff's lips:

'Since I pluck'd geese,' said he, 'play'd truant, and whipp'd top, I knew not what t'was to be beaten, till lately.'

A handkerchief rolled tightly, we found, made a good ball for 'rounders'. Sometimes we got a real ball. Our teachers took very little interest in our games. We did not blame them. Their duty, as far as we knew, was to impart geography, and stuff our little minds with English and arithmetic. The master sometimes picked up a rounder-bat when he came out to wash his hands at the pump after lunch. We thought that wonderful.

The school provided one great rope for skipping; otherwise we were left completely alone.

Hop-scotch came and went. For weeks we played 'Houses' round tree-trunks and protruding roots.

Once a year we had a wedding down the back road. Near our school gate was a tall aisle of hawthorn. And never did man or nature contrive anything happier for confetti than the round white petals of hawthorn.

I walked into a great city shop some time ago, and the young man behind the counter looked up with a smile to ask: 'Do you remember when we were married down under the hawthorn?' 'Of course I do.' 'But in the meantime,' I was forced to add, 'I seem to have lost sight of my bridegroom.' We laughed.

Year after year, in blossom-time, the senior girl was the bride, draped shyly in a window-curtain, and the senior boy, as suitably 'attired' in a white buttonhole was the bridegroom. Others shared the honours of the occasion as bridesmaids and flower girls. It was all very simple.

We got permission that day to lunch out of the playground, and found a place to set out our lunch as a wedding-feast on the quiet roadside. One of the big girls brought from home a 'fair linen cloth'. The smell of bruised grass in springtime, and the clean, strong fragrance of hawthorn still have power to call up for me that happy hour.

All our pleasures were as simple.

And our sins were as simple. The only time I got the strap at school was along with eleven others, for stealing turnips. We didn't steal them, we said, we just took them. Mr. Tasker had plenty; his sheep were eating them. It was rather too much to expect that Mr. Tasker would appreciate our point of view. He came up to school and made a fuss, and our master, who had never strapped us, had to do something about it. We didn't blame him—it wasn't his fault; we didn't even blame ourselves. We blamed Mr. Tasker!

Time was big then. There was time in which to dream—and a whole eternity before us in which to do things.

Our first musical instrument made its appearance at

school when we were about ten. Till then we knew no music, save our simple songs unaccompanied, the black-bird fluting in the garden at dusk, and the thrush with his

'Toodle-too, toodle-too, toodle-too!
E acute, E acute, E acute!'

It was a memorable day when our parents bought an Edison phonograph. It stood on a three-legged table in a corner of the 'front room', and had an unwieldy horn like an overgrown convolvulus blossom. It played *The Blue Danube*, and *On Wings of Song*. Neighbouring farmers came for miles on winter nights to listen to it, travelling in their traps. We saved up as we could to buy cylinders. But when the piano came, it gradually fell into disuse.

The coming of the piano was a great event, so that for years afterwards we dated things as from 'the year before we got the piano', or 'the year we got the piano'.

Our father and a farmer friend brought it home in the wagonette, and with coats off, and faces red, pulled down the side fence to get it in.

A neighbour had an organ with a pleated silk front and brass candle-sticks. Our piano wasn't like that—we were sorry it wasn't. When our father, wiping his brow, stood off appraising it, he said it was 'plain, but good'.

After the first exciting days of possession, it stood in solitary grandeur in the sacred 'front room'.

Then word reached us, by way of the butcher, that Mrs. Biggar 'could take us'. That meant that our musical education was about to begin.

Our music teacher—the only one in miles—was a widow, with two lads, and an old mother to support. She lived in one of the two white earth cottages in the village, and biked all over the country on an outrageously squeaky bicycle—no compliment to her ear as a teacher of music. And she had no idea of the passing of the hours.

Sometimes, she would be heard approaching far off

SC—B*

after we children had gone to bed, and we would have to get up, in turn, and put on coats over our nighties, and sit beside her.

I was stubborn. I hope I didn't age her before her time, but it must soon have become plain to her that there was no future for me in Czerny's Exercises. I wanted to play the violin. My father had a violin. But it was no use. Persuasively but firmly my father and mother said: 'No, not yet. Do what you can with the piano first—it will help you—learn to read music and time.' But it was no use.

My sister made good progress. Soon she was playing little pieces of Schubert's. They sounded wonderful to us. I suspect now that they might not have sounded so wonderful to Schubert.

Like most children, I had any amount of perseverance for things that I did care about. I once copied out the whole of one of Dickens's stories, because we only had a battered copy, and I wanted my friends at school to read it.

I was heroic, too—I was always rescuing people. I was Joan of Arc, and Elizabeth Fry, and Florence Nightingale all rolled into one.

I biked all over the countryside collecting for Dr. Barnardo's Homes, in a London I had only read about in Dickens. I got a white medal for collecting, and a bronze one. Whatever it did for the waifs and strays, it broadened my sympathies; and a new kind of courage fastened itself upon me when out collecting. For the rest, I was frightfully shy, save in the little world where I was sure of myself—the very little world of school and home, and the green world of trees and hedges. My father and mother did their best, but I was almost in my teens before I would go willingly to a meal away from home. To sit opposite a stranger was almost more than I could bear. My favourite essayist has confessed to a like shyness. It stayed with him well up into his twenties. 'At one of the houses to which I carried an introduction,' said E. V. Lucas, 'there used to be plenty to listen to. I say *listen*, for I was much too shy to take part . . . In consequence of this shyness, I must confess to having allowed several Sundays to pass before I could collect enough courage to ring the bell.'

My troubles began when someone else rang the bell, and I was never really happy until I heard the gate click, and they were gone.

'On one occasion,' confessed E. V. L., 'I went all the way down to Kensington . . . starving, and then daren't face the ordeal of meeting strangers. No one, who is not shy,' he finished, 'can have any notion of the odds with which the shy have to contend, and the bitter struggles they pass through.'

IV

In summer holiday-times there was always a place for me in the fields. Sometimes at night I felt I might fall asleep unlacing my boots.

Those who know the countryside only from occasional visits think of hay-making and corn-harvesting as the most pleasant times of the year. They are pleasant times, but they are also times of hard work, feverish haste and anxiety. Will the weather last? Will the rain come before the crop can be got in? Is it better to risk the weather than the possibility that the hay will sweat in the stack?

To one who likes farming there is great satisfaction in it, but it is the 'everydayness' of it that defeats those who do not like it. If you are an office-worker, you can sometimes forget it, but you can never forget that you are a farmer.

I accompanied my father in the fields. We picked up the ripe sheaves as they fell from the binder—an ancient, paintless, respected thing. It was hot work. Round and round the field it went, and we could never catch up, for all we sweated and toiled.

How good our jug of lemon-juice tasted in the mid-morning! When we had taken our fill my father and I turned proudly again to our work. The remainder of the large jug we left, with its couple of mugs, under the sweet shelter of a stook.

Our stooks were of eight sheaves—four on each side, standing proudly in the sunlight. After my father had drawn my attention to it, I could see that the butt end of a sheaf wasn't level. It sloped. This made a great difference to whether stooks stood up, or fell down. It was a matter of pride to have your stooks all standing in the morning after a night of summer wind or rain. There was a knack in it. Grasping a sheaf under each arm, we clumped them together on the ground simultaneously, with the shorter sides of the butts together. Almost in the same action we locked the ears a little.

Our stooks had to regard the prevailing winds, as they stood tent-like, with the little tunnel through the middle.

I started my stooking with oats—oats were lighter to handle than wheat or barley. Wheat was especially heavy, and barley had a beard of raspy whiskers on each stalk. Taken separately, they were harmless enough, but together, they rasped bare legs and arms. I never liked barley. When it dried, the little whiskers broke off, and got into one's hair, and up one's sleeves. They were respectfully known as 'barley-iles'.

It was a healthy toil! And at night I was often so tired I might have tumbled into bed with all my clothes on, and never noticed it.

Later, when the sheaves came in from the fields, I 'crowed' on the stack. Neighbouring farmers came in to help. We needed always an extra dray and driver.

My father built his own stack, down on his knees on the sweet dry sheaves, that a week or so earlier we had stooked in the fields. And I 'crowed'—I received the sheaves, as one by one they were hurled up on to his growing stack, and forked them across to where he was working.

Many and many a time I felt I couldn't hold on a minute longer. The sun was so fierce. But always then, the next dray was late in coming, or the home-folk would appear with the lunch, and I was saved. I was strong, and proud of my young strength. I didn't want my father to think I couldn't do a job.

I even learned to load a dray—to build the front higher than the back, so that the load would ride well and not slip as we moved over the rough stubble.

It was a day of special pride when my father let me help him thatch a stack. Old Dicky Palmer's stacks were the best in the district—neat and shapely—and I always thought my father's came next. It was an occasion for mirth when a farmer built a stack, and so misjudged his job that he had to prop it up with long lengths of wood till the thresher came.

The thatch-pegs—little finger-thick sticks—were kept from year to year. Every season we had to gather fresh rushes. In areas where rushes were scarce, dry rye or wheat-straw was used. Deftly placed, and pegged, with a length of twine from peg to peg, the natural varnish on the stalks helped to turn the rain.

My fellow-country-woman, Katherine Mansfield, was right when she said: '*The more I see of life the more I feel that it's the people who live remote from cities who inherit the earth.*'

But all these delights of earth were suddenly threatened when I was about twelve.

On either side of our village flowed a river, converging a little below us, at what had been the 'old Snowden farm'. And in the village was an inventor—a clever inventor—a little gnome-like brown-faced man with a merry chuckle of laughter. But he had, the village people said, a way of 'tying things up with bits of string'. He owned the Flour Mill, and thanks to him, our village had electric light long before the town of Nelson.

Away up the river that fed his Flour Mill (and farther down, our beloved Flax Mill) he built a dam. It was of concrete and seemed, to the casual observer, strong enough. But one autumn the rivers flooded. The waters brought down with them great logs and debris from the Gorge. And the dam could not take it.

Of a sudden we knew the worst—the great barricade of concrete gave way and down came the wall of water.

As the great waters rushed on, breaking the railway-bridge and embankment, much of our farm was carried off down the river.

The desolation was accompanied by a high wind. It blew the top off our cart-shed, and up-ended it. As the waters rose, our fowls, in terror, flew up on to that seeming place of safety. Next minute, down it came, and they were being carried along in the turbulent waters toward the house. Outside our kitchen was a paling-fence. We flung up the window, and rescued those we could. The paling-fence acted as a strainer as the waters bore down upon it, and apples, pumpkins, pieces of board, old boots and all sorts of rubbish piled up against it.

The horses, terrified and separated from us by the gulf of water, took refuge on the half-blown-down straw-stack. Outside our front door—in Palmer's paddock, where we had mushroomed—were dotted little islands of life. Gradually, as one was overwhelmed, sheep took to the swirling waters in an effort to reach a higher spot. Outside ones on each little island were gradually swept away. In a short time, a number of islands had gone altogether. At last, only a handful of the several hundred sheep were safe on a knob, the highest land as far as the eye could see. And still the waters were rising. By lunch-time we had several inches—a foot almost—in our dairy. Ten minutes later, the wheel-barrow had gone, full of next morning's kindling.

But this tragedy was not without its humours. When things were at their worst my sister silently retired to the sacred 'front-room' to pick out on the piano the old hymn: '*Master, the tempest is raging!*'

43

It was raging—and it raged until the whole of Bateup's orchard next door was up-rooted, and every fence was down in miles.

Nobody knew quite what to do at first. As the waters receded, the immediate concern was the damage that had been done. Then came the heart-breaking task of burying the animals that had been caught in fences and trees.

Gradually our father and our neighbours rose from their blow, and began to make plans. For days and days that stretched into weeks, they went together down the river-bed to bring back what they could of the farms, *a dray-load at a time*. It was a heart-breaking business.

Who wanted to stay on a farm that next season might be washed down the river? But who wanted to give a good price to purchase such a farm?

My father went about a quiet, thoughtful man those days. And a change came. At what cost I suppose I little guessed. We moved to the village.

We children felt from the first that we were lucky to get the old two-storied house at the cross-ways. Certainly its garden was a wilderness, but there were interesting old trees, and five acres of land. On the other three corners were the old doctor's home, the Methodist chapel, and the wheelwright's. The village was laid out in the form of a cross—with the church at one end, and the hotel at the other. In between was a higgle-piggle of houses.

One compensation to me was that on our property was a blacksmith's shop. There, week in, week out, the great farm-horses from miles around came to be shod. I spent a lot of time at that blacksmith's shop. Things happened there.

In the winter, especially, when birds' nests were forgotten, and thoughts of the river and fields were laid away, the blacksmith's shop came into its own. In the summer there was little time to spare for this 'stygian cave of wonders', unless some implement needed the blacksmith's skill. In the winter it was different. We knew the call of home in the winter, with its little room where we stored the apples, and its rambly garden and blacksmith's yard. It was called 'the blacksmith's yard' though it belonged to father, and our wood-pile stood there.

Many a time, under my breath, I thanked God for that wood-pile, and the excuse it gave me to be near that enchanting spot. The wood split—and I loved splitting wood, especially willow and pine, for their sweet smells— it was the easiest thing in the world to slip into that smithy.

The blacksmith started early. All the year round, before I had risen, I could hear the musical sound of his hammer on the anvil.

The smithy itself was a low building with an earthen floor, where the great horses came to stamp and whinny. The bellows blew, the sparks flew upwards, the leather-aproned bare-armed smith made the anvil ring out its double or single song.

On wet days it was especially warm and friendly there. The earthen floor under one's feet seemed primeval and satisfying, and there were wonderful things on hand. Wet days were the blacksmith's busiest days. The men, finding little to do on the farm, once their tools were in order, and empty sacks mended, came about mid-morning to the blacksmith's shop. They tied their great horses in the blacksmith's yard where our wood-pile stood, or in the front area behind the stout rail that shut off the sacred precincts from the common road outside. Making myself inconspicuous, I heard much good sense talked there. My favourite spot was at the bellows, where I could make myself useful, hour after hour, to save being turned out.

The tinkle of the hammer on the anvil of the forge is a

joy unknown to many. Besides the shoeing of the horses, and the mending of farm implements, the smith made beautiful things like fire-irons and gates. The sturdy gates that gave entrance to our chapel were made at his anvil.

On odd days he taught me how to heat two irons, and with tongs bring them from the glow when they turned a pinky chrome yellow, and weld them on the anvil with deft hammer blows.

Sometimes we did a more thrilling thing. Instead of mending, we made things that had never been before. I have still in my possession a hammer that I made under the kindly eye of the smith. I doubt whether I could buy a better one, certainly I could never buy one that would give me such joy to handle.

The passing of the blacksmith with his craft of bellows, forge and anvil, is a great loss to the poetry of the country-side. The old smithy that stood at the centre of my life for several years, as the place where lovely things were made, has long since been closed and shuttered.

Mechanical farming, mass production, and the rapid popularity of the motor, have brought repercussions to the village blacksmith. To-day, the plough, harrow and drill must move behind the tractor, at a speed impossible to horses.

But the significance of anvil and forge remain part of our literature and our living. Only this morning I turned up a passage in Isaiah: 'Behold, I have created the smith that bloweth the coals in the fire, and that bringeth forth an instrument for his work.' And I am glad of that word as background to the dignity of an honest workman.

After birds'-nesting, the first money I earned in the village was pay from the wheelwright. He was also the undertaker. And in the absence of 'his man', he paid me half-a-crown for painting an old man's coffin-plate—his age, name and date.

V

FATHER and mother dearly loved a garden. The world's first contest we are told, was staged in a garden. I can well believe it, for many a friendly contest was staged in ours.

Close by our house was a special plot of soil, sheltered and sunny—bordered on one side by a path, on another by an old-fashioned windmill, and a flourishing fig-tree. At one point, the vegetables and flowers met. And that frontier, I believe, was as many times challenged as any frontier in changeable Europe. It was my mother's seasonal policy to push it back—if not by peaceful penetration, then by open invasion.

On those few occasions when my father got in first with his season's row of cabbages, there was an armed truce. But no cabbage can hold its own on the frontier for ever. Time and our culinary needs compelled him to evacuate his forces. And before he could bring up reinforcements, my mother had made a swift sortie and thrown into the gap a battalion of poppies.

My father took up his new position again and again; but at last he dug himself in permanently with a long line of spikey gooseberry bushes.

Every time I pick up Sir John Simon's *Portrait of My Mother*, I am sorry that he did not publish it until 1936. 'Our garden at Bath,' says Sir John, with happy recollections, 'was only a small one, and my mother grudged the space that was taken up with kitchen vegetables. Her husband, who believed in making practical use of much of the ground, found one morning that she had been out as soon as it was light, in order to appropriate a coveted corner, and had nailed up on the trunk of an adjoining

47

pear-tree, the text, with Bible reference complete: "Cursed be he who removeth his neighbour's landmark".'

That would have pleased my mother!

We had been only a little time in the village when I had to spend weeks, stretching into months, indoors.

It was my mother's custom before the evening meal to attend to her day's supply of cream in the tiny dairy. Just on dusk one evening she called for a pot of boiling water. I feigned deafness—a common and useful discovery of preoccupied youth—but in the end, my better nature won. I went to the kitchen to fetch the pot of boiling water, and on my way back slipped, and spilled it.

By the time my mother could unlace my boot, and drag off my thick stocking, it was plain I was badly scalded.

The next nights and days I do not remember—save that when I came out of my delirium it was to find my mother and father beside me, and to realize that the house was quiet. Sometimes the old doctor was there. For some reason he chose to incise the blisters that formed, letting in cold, unkind air on to the raw flesh.

Winter drew on. And that year I was absent from my countryside in the spring. It was unthinkable that birds should build, and I not there to see.

For months the old doctor continued to come, to mutter a few words, and to go away.

The scar of my burn I have still. It marks a time when a new seriousness entered my 'long, long thoughts of youth'. Till then I had been as little conscious of my body as a young, wild thing.

When I could hobble about again my blacksmith friend brought me a leather apron of the sort he wore, and made me a bandage slipper to go over my dressings.

After a time I found I could pedal one foot on a bicycle.

It was a fixed-wheel machine, and served me well, but it was a weary business. I feared my disability would swing the balances between our little old school and the village school. Since we had moved, we had a couple of extra miles to go, and had to pass the village school on the way.

I was right—the break came, and I hated it.

The little old school under the great trees, stood for much in my life. The interest factor is spoken of these days as though it were something new. But is there anything new about it, except the jargon?—'that the urge toward creative ideation in the adolescent is primarily volitional'. Surely old Ascham, in his *Schole-Master* away back in 1550, understood that, and said it much more beautifully: 'Liberty kindleth love: and love requireth no labour.' Certainly we understood it, without ever giving it a name.

The class into which I was drafted in the new school was disorderly, and in the midst of its term's work. Often in those days I lifted up my eyes to the clock.

At the end of the year I went with a handful of others to the village of Wakefield to sit my proficiency exam. My shy pride that day was in the paintings I was allowed to take with me. For several years, whilst the drawing lesson was going on at school, I had been allowed to bike up to a tiny studio at the back of the village library. It reeked of raw linseed oil, but it was heaven to me, *for I meant to be an artist*.

'Oh, the enthusiasm of the first glowing sunrise of ideals!'

My father bought me a beautiful box of paints. I have it still. He loved good tools. When I passed my proficiency exam, he bought me a camera. And I have that still. All the illustrations in this book were made with it. My father seldom made a gift, but when he did, he chose always something that one could learn to handle and treasure through the years. In this deeply-instilled hatred of shoddy stuff our mother supported him.

Another far-reaching thing that my father and mother did—and did so naturally—was to balance in my life the artistic and the practical. If I fell in love with a poem, I had also to peel apples for a pie; if I learned a new song, I learned also to half-sole a pair of shoes; if I went into ecstasies over a sunset, I had also to dust the front sitting-room. One result was that to me a life unrelated to the comings and goings of normal existence has always been suspect. I have never been able to sustain interest in saints who could only be saints by going apart from life, or in artists and writers who could only create in a rarefied air. I have never been able to escape the feeling that those who would teach me about life, *must first of all know how to live.*

At the turn of the school year I should have gone on to College—but my secondary education had gone down the river. I went to work instead.

For my labours in the village store I received fifteen shillings a week. Three-parts of it went to my mother for my keep.

But at the end of the front veranda there was a little un-used room. I took possession of it, and got a key. When I had saved to buy rolls of wallpaper, my mother made me a bucket of paste. I stained the floor, and bound my little old piece of red carpet. I built bookshelves, and an up-right chair. I hung my modest pictures. As Hazlitt says: 'There is a feeling of eternity in youth which makes us amends for everything. To be young is to be one of the immortals.'

I had good company there. I got to know Whittier and

Keats and Lamb. As the years passed I cut a trail for myself through the thickets of English literature. I read the Authorized Version—'the best words set in the best order during the best period of our language'. I dug into English grammar, theology, and history. Night after night, the hours flew on toward eleven; but the little sounds would come creeping back—the clock ticking softly, bits of wood falling out of the fire, the cat breathing in its sleep. I would lay my books away, and creep on slippered feet through the house and, save for the creaky seventh stair, quietly to bed.

I valued greatly my power to read, for in the village were two people denied that privilege. I saw what limitations were theirs. One of them—Old Lizzie—was a law-abiding old soul who went out cleaning and got up every morning by an '*alarmin*' clock'. But if ever my mother sought her help, it could never be on a Thursday. Her reply was always the same: 'Can't come on a Thursday, Mrs. Snowden, my dear. That's the day I go down to the vicarage with the Guild, to sew for the leopards. 'The leopards' we knew as 'Lepers'—the responsibility of the church on a little palm-fringed island of the Pacific.

The other whom I knew well was a work-mate of my father's when he left the farm. One day, a small boy following his father at the plough, drank plough-oil from a bottle at the end of the furrow, and died. Reporting the tragedy, our old friend said to my father when next they met: 'I see they held a *portmanteau* over Ab's boy.' That evening our little paper reported the *post-mortem* examination.

The only villager who ever came to my little den was a lover of books. She did a clerical job in the village, and led a Sunday-class of young folk—Brethren, like herself, Anglican, Methodist, Baptist. Her methods were not always the latest, and some of her theology I had to unlearn—but she loved life, and she loved laughter. She lifted religion out of a negative atmosphere, and made it a positive thing. I owe her an everlasting debt. Trees and skies she loved, too. Out of work hours, we went long jaunts together.

Then when I was nearing thirteen a travelling evangelist came to the village. With my folk I had attended the Methodist church from the beginning, affectionately known as 'the Chapel'. I was almost never absent from our pew, though no one guessed the thoughts that were in my mind. I was suffering from spiritual growing-pains.

The thoughts of a growing boy or girl baffle expression. We have words to describe outward objects, and common sensations like joy and pain. But when we come to find words for the strange thoughts that visit us, the response to our environment, our feeling about the unknown, we are at a loss.

I knew—to put it in the language of the local-preachers who came—that I was 'not right with God'; but nobody ever seemed to say in as plain words how I could be, until I came to think that perhaps it was like finding out where babies came from, a thing one had to find out for oneself.

With most of the villagers I attended the evangelistic mission. I was shy, the atmosphere was tense. I refused to be 'stormed' into the Kingdom, and yet I knew I couldn't hold back.

All the while I struggled. My mind refused to join its assent to my emotions. But it was only a matter of time. In the quietness of my little 'den', and as suddenly as release came to Saul upon the Damascus Road, and to Saul Kane, in Masefield's *Everlasting Mercy*, it came to me. Taking the place of that long torment of mind, and laborious piling up of 'good works', I heard Our Lord's words from the Cross: '*It is finished!*'

From that moment I was a new creature. I felt people would surely know that something had happened to me; I felt there was a shine upon the very skin of my face. I was still too shy, and too happy to speak of it to my elders, but I sought out a young friend, who attended the Anglican church, and tried to put into stumbling words the thing that had happened to me. We went a long bike ride, and our tiny lamps failed, and we walked home. In the darkness, my shyness took leave of me.

Two mornings later, as I was sweeping out the store, I received a note from my friend, and knew the joy, unmatched on this earth, of sharing my faith with another.

> *The earth and every common sight*
> *To me did seem*
> *Apparelled in celestial light:*
> *The glory and the freshness of a dream.*

Explain it? I could not then, and I cannot fully now, any more than I can explain the coming of the dawn. It was a miracle, and it touched my life. It is not easy to find words to hold down such reality, and I'm not sure that it matters—*the whole of life is left for that.*

I set about refashioning my plans. I was still at the store. I sought comfort in Carlyle's words that 'the true university is a good collection of books'. I knew that it didn't cover the whole situation, however confidently quoted; academic recognition, I saw, I should never be granted—the store stood in the way of that—but I hoped that someday I might be an educated person.

I added to my books, I wrestled with my correspondence course. Somewhere, I felt there must be a tutor who would say to me the kind of things Ernest Raymond's old master said to him: 'I don't care two-pence about giving you *facts*—the official in the next class-room can do that—and

53

anybody can remember facts. I'm going to give you ideas. I don't think it matters much if the ideas are right, so long as you *think* and *feel*. I don't want to teach you to know, but to interpret. See? Any fool can know. *Wisdom comes when you begin to interpret.*'

VI

I STAYED six years at the store—and years are long in youth. It did something for me for which I am thankful. It taught me in measure to surmount my shyness. It brought me into touch with people—village people, and people of the wide countryside.

It was an interesting store—one of four owned by the same family, before chain-stores were a feature of trade. It served the countryside before the advent of farmers' cars, which now rush past it to the town half-an-hour's drive away. Farmers and farmers' wives drove up in their gigs and farm-carts, and never thought of going farther.

We served them with groceries and barbed wire, plough-oil and fruit sprays, and all that they could need out-of-doors. We bought their butter and eggs, and smoked their bacon; we furnished their rooms; we kept a shelf of books in an effort to furnish their minds. Our stock of hats and ties helped to keep them self-conscious.

We saw life as it was lived; we knew those who were 'good pays', and those who were not. We knew those who tried to cheat on the weight of their butter, and those who bought too much 'tin-stuff', and fed on things they couldn't afford.

We took down the shutters at eight, six mornings a week, and kept them down till six in the evening—nine on Fridays. Saturdays was a cherished half-holiday, after one o'clock. Christmas Eve was the year's big event. Then we kept open till eleven, and played assistant to Santa Claus with all the secrecy demanded by the occasion. On New Year's Eve we celebrated again, with every man, woman and child who could be of the crowd and join in the fun.

We gave our share of service, and did our share of grumbling; we saw interesting sidelights on human nature, and enjoyed them together over morningtea.

After a number of years, the business changed hands. Our vanman and Aberdonian accountant took it over on shares; but the vanman continued his perambulations round the countryside, and we fell to the mercy of our old bachelor. He was lame and short, and used a stick; and he wore on his bald pate a handsome little black smoking-cap, and greeted the faults and failings of humanity with great impatience. He read well, attended worship on the Sabbath, and wrote weekly to his two elderly spinster sisters in Scotland; but there were some things he did not know.

Among our customers were certain wives from distant farms, who, when they came down, could never resist our display. They might find it difficult to choose between two pieces of dress-material, and decide to take them both— one for immediate use, and one to put by. This practice had a tendency to spread, and to drag on accounts from month to month. And our old Aberdonian was all against it.

One day, one of our worst offenders came down. Among other requests, she asked to see a pair of corsets. The long, slender boxes were brought down from the shelves, and she made her choice. Corsets were corsets in those days, and her purchase was duly laced up, and entered up: 'Mrs. T. W. B., one pair of corsets 16s. 6d.'

Next morning, when our old accountant was going through the books, he came upon the entry. Sparing it no more than a glance, he grabbed up his stick, jammed on his little smoking-cap more determinedly, and hobbled out. 'Miss Snawden, Miss Snawden, look here!' he

56

cried, slamming the book down on the counter. 'What does this mean? Mrs. T. W. B., one pair of cossits, sixteen-and-six. B-l-a-s-t the woman, b-l-a-s-t the woman. Didn't you tell her? What does she want with a *pair* of cossits? Why wouldn't *one* do?'

And to me fell the embarrassing task of explaining that much as one bought a pair of shoes, or a pair of braces, one bought a pair of corsets.

No one in our home bought anything on time-payment. Our father and mother had a contemptuous word for it: '*Tick!*'

The first thing I ever saved for was a bicycle—and it took me months and months to save for that gleaming miracle done up in long strips of hessian.

Before her marriage, our mother had owned the first lady's *free-wheel* bicycle in Nelson. All our childhood we had revelled in the story of how she had to leave it in the shop on show for months after she had bought it. How she managed to restrain her urgent joy of possession, I could never think.

In the interval she had the tailor make for her a hand-some divided-skirt. It was of a fashionable khaki colour, with little gold buttons down the front. And when she appeared, people said: 'Oh, there she goes! There she goes!' And to others: 'Oh, you're just too late—you've just missed her!'

I never saw that beautiful bicycle, but I got into trouble for my share in cutting up that handsome volumi-nous skirt *to make a soldier uniform for a teddy-bear*! It was ideal for the purpose—with its little gold buttons. Our mother had been saving it up for years, to clothe her twins when the opportunity arrived. It was a sorry sight when she came upon it.

After the sweet liberty that came with my bicycle, our ten-year-old brother was next to take to himself wheels. But he was a child of the new age bursting in upon our life. He got himself a motor-bike, a 'B.A.T.' It had lain under rubbish in our bachelor uncle's shed since it had broken down.

With commendable ingenuity the young mechanic pulled it to bits and put it together again. For weeks after he began on it, our mother looked on anxiously. 'Look at your clothes, boy,' she would say, 'and look at your knees, and your socks!'

Always the same answer was forthcoming: 'But look, I've nearly got her to go. Only one more thing to do, and she'll go—and I know how to do it!'

Blessed youth with enthusiasms! Blessed mothers with patience!

Then one Saturday, it did go—to the delight of the family, and the consternation of 'Rosie' and 'Blackie' in the cow-paddock.

The good news spread, and schoolboys in twos and threes and half-dozens came for a ride on the back of the 'B.A.T.' The young mechanic was not old enough to get a licence to ride on the road, so they had to be satisfied to ride round the cow-paddock. The motor-man in the village, it was discovered, could supply benzine in lemonade-bottles at threepence a time. All was well while there was pocket-money, but there were grim days when threepences gave out. Then three or four schoolboys might be seen squatting on the top of our big five-barred gate, chins in hands, like a row of disconsolate sparrows.

When harvest came in mid-December, everybody in the village was glad of a pair of wheels. There was no social stigma about helping in the harvest-fields—the schoolmaster's wife, the shop-keeper's son and the black-smith's daughter all toiled together.

The peas came first. Picking peas was hard work and dull. The gradient was steep where the earliest peas grew. Every morning, lunch slung over our shoulders, we biked to Max's peas, before the sun was hot. Then we dismounted, and prepared for the long day's work. A boy belonging to the farm was detailed to sledge us up to the top where the picking began. We liked that. And then dragging our buckets, and sitting on our boots, we worked our way down. The sun beat down mercilessly as the day wore on. The buckets were heavy to drag, and the distance between where we picked, and the loose hessian bags into which we put the peas, seemed endless. It took five well-filled buckets to fill a bag; and for that amount of back-aching effort, we got one-and-sixpence! A good picker could manage five bags a day, sometimes six. We young people were well-pleased if our record was four.

When we picked on the Plains, it was even more wearisome. The ground was covered with flat hot stones, that by midday were painful to squat on.

Another back-aching job was picking up wind-falls in the orchards. It was a poorly paid job and an unpleasant one, when the bees and wasps sat on broken fruit. But we rated it higher than pea-picking, because there was some shelter from the fierce sun.

After plums came early apricots—and we were quickly and fully launched into what Keats called the 'mellow fruitfulness'.

Picking apples was a task reserved for the strongest and most careful amongst us. It involved moving a ladder, as well as a hessian bag of fruit round one's waist. Even the strongest of us found it heavy work. 'There were ten thousand thousand fruit to touch, cherish in hand, lift down, and not let fall.' And when I got home at night my feet not only kept the ache, they kept also the pressure of a ladder-rung.

Late in the autumn came hops. We had Kentish hops, but unlike the hop-picking in Kent, it carried no social stigma with us. In our little world hop-picking stood high in the estimation of those who did it. Once again the schoolmaster's wife and the shop-keeper's daughter worked side by side. Those who camped away looked upon it more as a holiday with pay. But there was always bother with those who had to pick the outside rows. They were wind-whipped and tangled. One year, I remember, the old hop-grower came smilingly to tell us that he'd got over the difficulty—he wasn't going to have any more grumbling—*he'd taken out the outside row!*

Those of us who had hop-gardens near, left in the early morning on our bikes, returning weary and bine-stained in the evening. It was a healthy life. Good appetites were quickened at the great hessian bins.

But changes were coming. I think our young brother only once went to the hop-gardens. I doubt whether he ever went picking peas. He was only seven years behind us, but those seven years, when he was ready to leave school, seemed to bridge the old life and the new.

The river, with its great weeping willows and gliding green pools, was never to him the joy it had been to me. And the mill, with its murmuring wheel, and little water-fall over henna-red willow-root, was never to him the enchanting spot that it was to me. The old rowing-boat belonging to the mill, was all my childhood like an extension of my personality.

By the time our brother was in his 'teens, another flood had changed the course of our swimming-pool, and then the mill was burned down. I never cared to go there after that.

But the greatest changes were the mechanical changes that were coming into the world of young and old alike. I doubt whether our brother ever rode behind a

A TREE SENTINEL ABOVE A CITY

(*Adelaide*)

horse, except as a child in arms. His thoughts all ran to speed.

I had been still at school when the first motor-car in our district appeared. An old chain-drive, it made a terrific noise, and emitted bad smells. The first I knew of its existence, I was coming home alone. Still believing a little in storybook dragons, I got through a five-wire fence into a field of corn. I remember—so vividly was that moment impressed upon me—that in that field there were wild white violets and shivery-grass. I crouched among them until the terrifying thing had gone past. Its driver and lady passenger—man and wife—sat bolt upright and the lady wore a wide purple motoring-veil.

But before our brother was out of his 'teens, far from escaping into a field of barley, he was enthusing over our own family car. I doubt whether he knew that such wonders as shivery-grass existed: I doubt whether he ever lay on his back in the summer watching the clouds, or closer still, the little ladybirds, and funny little unnameable things that ran up and down the grass stalks. He had to go from here to there, and in the quickest way. He had to save five minutes, and *spend ten minutes boasting how he'd saved them.*

By the time he was ready for college, the telephone and electric light were common enough, and the movie-film and the wireless had come. I shall never forget the night when we crowded in to see our first film. After a promising start, for some reason it became temperamental, and then broke down, and we had to sit in the dark. I remember my father saying: 'These pictures will never take on; people will never put up with sitting in the dark.'

A neighbouring farmer had the first wireless-set we knew, and we tramped across at night to sit hushed in his kitchen taking turns with the ear-phones. The first night, I remember, we heard nothing but scratchings and scrapings. The next night, wonder of wonders, we heard a man's voice—heard it say one or two words—all the way from Wellington, nearly a hundred miles away.

But by the time our brother was finished with college, we had a set of our own, and all the world came in for better or worse.

Then the first aeroplane came to Nelson. We went with others to a paddock to meet it. But it was hours late, and when it did come, it landed in a hayfield a few minutes from our home. So little was known of its possible behaviour, that a neighbouring schoolmaster spent the morning up on the school-roof to be the first to see it come. So little we knew. Nobody knew whether we should first hear it and then see it, whether we should see it first and then hear it, or whether it might suddenly appear through the cloud above our heads.

Our young brother belonged to the new age. He thought easily in terms of 'planes, movies, and motors. He went in and out to college every day—thirteen miles off— and when he was ready to be apprenticed to a trade, he found that trade thirteen miles off, and motored in and out. His entertainment he found there, and his friends he made there, or at an equal distance off in some other direction.

All these marvels of modern science I have since made use of many times, but I am glad to have lived in a world where these were not. A child had time then to think, and to wonder: and a child needs a lot of time for that. All over the world then little children could kneel and say their prayers and go to bed without fear. Their homes would be safe about them in the morning—none were then blasted to rubble overnight.

I have since spent years in cities—some of them the great cities of the world—but I have still a country heart. When the sap rises and the buds come, the old call is still there.   I understand completely V. Sackville-West's feeling about city people:

> *Book-learning they have known.*
> *They meet together, talk, and grow most wise,*
> *But they have lost, in losing solitude,*
> *Something—an inward grace, the seeing eyes,*
> *The power of being alone.*
> *The power of being alone with earth and skies,*
> *Of going about a task with quietude,*
> *Aware at once of earth's surrounding mood*
> *And of an insect crawling on a stone.*

VII

Our setting was small—small enough to be intimate, but not small enough to be insignificant. It was something to know everyone—to be able to salute as friends the butcher, the grocer, the village simpleton and the vicar's wife.

Its green-backed hills and blue mountains remain beyond it to-day, and as faithful as ever, though much has changed. Tall spiring poplars with delicate tops of green still stand tip-toe in the spring, and my father still enjoys them. But—and how often there is a 'but' as the years go by—my mother is not there.

Always when I go back, folk speak of her—and oddly, in one breath, of her Sunday-school, and her apron. I say 'oddly', but really it was the most natural thing. I hardly remember her without her cleanly fresh apron. It has its place in my last sight of her, as I left home for the first time, and in the first glimpse I caught of her as she welcomed me back at the end of term; and when, with half-an-hour's warning, she left us at the close of a day we shall always remember, she was wearing her apron.

Curiosity getting the better of me, I once opened my dictionary—'that enemy of mystery, destroyer of charm'—as one has called it, and let Mr. Webster tell me what is an apron. 'An apron,' he said, 'is a portion of cloth . . . worn as a protective covering in the front of one's person.

But I have an unhappy feeling that he knows little about it. I much prefer the judgement of Peter.

When we look back on those we love, it is usually to remember them by some everyday characteristic. So too when I think of my mother. She superintended a Sunday-school—not that she thought she was any great teacher;

but rather that in a small village there were few who cared to try. It was one of those simple things that happen in country places. Interest grew—it was bound to grow—and numbers grew. For miles around there was scarcely a child that ran unshepherded on Sunday mornings. Her own big class of boys surrounded her with a sort of shy comradeship, even after they were coming in their first long pants.

The week through she kept house—her tins full, her washing blowing early on the line on Monday morning, the butter turned out of her little yellow churn. She gave away bottles of milk to Sunday-school children who came from large families; jars from her precious preserve cupboard, and as a special treat, delicious black-currant jam in winter-time. In summer, it would be something else—fruit, bulging baskets filled with plums, ripe gooseberries, or any other of a dozen joys of a child's palate—and always with her apron on.

She didn't wear it to church or to Sunday-school—or, at least, I don't remember that she did—though it's a wonder, if only that she did it by mistake. But she wore the simple spirit of it there, as she wore it everywhere. In Dr. Moffatt's rendering of one of Peter's letters is the sort of thing I unconsciously set over thoughts of my mother: 'You must all put on the apron of humility to serve one another.'

'The apron of humility'—not a thing of cloth, oh no, but of a gentleness of spirit!

I was almost nineteen when a missionary came to the village, and talked to us about the Feeding of the Five Thousand. She gave it a fresh and striking interpretation. She made me see the people, set out on the grass, their garments as colourful as poppy beds. Their 'hundreds' and 'fifties', she said, represented the greater and lesser groupings of the world's peoples—some near at hand, some far away. They were all, she said, spiritually hungry —and there was food enough for all. The difficulty lay with the disciples responsible for the distribution. The tendency, as always at a picnic, was to over-feed the easily accessible, and leave the back ones to starve.

She gave us figures—told us how many Christians and churches we had, and how few they had in China, in Africa, in the islands of the sea.

The logic of it was unanswerable.

Already, it was true, I led a class of small boys, and collected for missions; already I organized fairs and concerts and Christmas trees. I led the Wesley Guild, sang in the choir, and spent days arranging lectures and concerts, and haranguing people to come and help. I did the church garden, and half-a-dozen times a year helped to scrub the church floor. When my mother's period of Sunday-school service came to an end I superintended in her stead.

But I was young—it seemed to me in the quietness of my little den that the Master stood beside me, reinforcing the challenge of that vision of the world I had seen, saying to me the same thing that He had said to those on that Galilean hillside: '*Go ye . . . !*' And all my little argument of unfitness, unworthiness, unwillingness was suddenly as nothing, in the presence of His assurance: 'And lo, I am with you always.'

Night after night the challenge held. Then I sat down and wrote a letter. When my minister received it, he put on his hat and cycled up to see me. There was a heavy gale blowing, and he had to walk most of the six miles. But he took me seriously—a very important thing in youth.

Under direction, I settled to more purposeful study, and

sat an exam.; and by the time I was nineteen I was enrolled as a prospective student at Methodist Deaconess House. Those who shared my interests in the village were at a loss to know why I wanted 'to run away from a job looking for a job'. *But I was young—and I saw the whole world in my vision.*

Christchurch, the southern city—my student home—I loved. Its English roots answered to something dimly understood in my heart. Its gardens I loved, and its limpid meandering river. I loved its sloping lawns with sprightly daisy rings down to the water's edge. And its trees—its gracious willows, their tresses hanging down like those of maidens in constant admiration. Its poplars I loved. And its old cathedral spire, rising central, with streets branching out, named after the English bishoprics —Gloucester, Manchester, Chester.

Methodist Deaconess House—'M.D.H.'—substantial behind its brass plate, looked out on to Latimer Square, as English as its name. At no great distance were two other tree-margined squares, bearing the names of the English martyrs, Ridley and Cranmer.

It was found that I had done my first-year text-books by correspondence, so I was switched on to second-year work. It was a good life. We rose early, and worked late. We learned, perhaps, as much of human nature from the training college and university students who shared the House with us, as from our lecturers.

Occasionally life took on sensational values, as when by night thieves stole the whole of our underwear from the line, and in a blushing moment we were summoned to the Police Station to identify the garments. And there was the weekly prayer-meeting, when we returned from the dignified stone church, by way of the pie-cart. And there was a winter night when the boiler overheated, and an innocent student, awakened by the noise, turned on all the taps to relieve the pressure. In a trice the nearby corridors were filled with steam, and twenty-five students leaped from beneath the blankets with the cry of 'Fire!'

For the rest, the only sensation might be a fellow-student in the corridor, before a psychology exam, mouthing her favourite definition of a sensation: 'A sensation is a psychical phenomenon resulting from the stimulation of the peripheral extremity of the afferent nerve when it is propagated to the brain.' It was harder to be a sensation in the exam-room, though it must still be somewhere recorded that I once got a hundred per cent for Church history. It was in my second year, and an embarrassment to me. I had firmly the impression that one ought not to reach perfection here, even in Church history. 'Couldn't the examiner have taken off a few marks for writing or spelling?' But the word was conclusive: 'He wasn't examining you in writing or spelling.' So I had to bear my hundred per cent. My fellow-students gave me a midnight supper, so no real harm was done.

As students, we discussed everything under the sun: 'The east, the west, the devil and the sunrise.' With us, it was no disgrace to be hard-up, but there were times when it was extremely inconvenient. The training college and 'varsity girls received pocket-money at the end of the month—though when I cut their hair at three-pence a time for missions, I had to wait for my dues. Deaconess students received no pocket-money; indeed, some of us contributed toward the cost of our training. One student did get *half-a-crown a month* from home, but usually it was mortgaged long before she got it. Shoes and stockings and the upkeep of our bicycles were the most constant drain on our resources. Everybody cycled in Christchurch—the gracious spready city held one of the world's records. We students were provided with uniforms—neat grey frocks, hats and tailored navy-blue coats. At first we were provided with Eton collars, linen bows and celluloid cuffs—very handy for taking pencil notes, if one found oneself without a pad—but in time, these were exchanged for turned-down linen collars, and badges. There still remained in the House a navy bonnet with satin ribbon and strings, which an earlier generation had rejoiced in—mute reminder of the evolution of our uniforms. Uniform, we saw, had it uses, even before we had won through to the right to wear full navy. It allowed us to be appropriately and smartly dressed on occasions of festivity or solemnity. In our work among children and the poor, it saved any comparison, and it was a protection, apart from providing us with what youth has always needed, a sign of authority.

I am pleased to remember now that when a design was needed for the badge of the Order, that submitted by my friend and myself was accepted—one simple triangle impressed upon another, symbolizing the dedication of body, mind and spirit, to God the Father, Son and Holy Spirit.

I was proud of our uniform. The precious rights of individuality didn't seem to matter then. There exists still in Quaker archives, I believe, an account book of Margaret Fox, which shows that even after she married George Fox, she once bought a scarlet gown. How she must have rejoiced in that gown! And Salvation Army historians treasure somewhere a picture of 'uncovenanted delight', when Mrs. William Booth and her daughter shut themselves up to try on bonnets of all shapes and sizes, before they could decide on the 'poke'.

As students we tried to keep mufti for off-duty hours, but swiftly and inevitably it got out of date. I could have sent home for money—but I was fashioned in an

SG.—C*

independent mould. In a specially tight corner, once I pawned my mufti hat. I got *five shillings* for it, which was little enough considering the careful planning and courage it took to pick a time when no one would see me go out through the gate with a paper hat-bag—or worse, return without it. If the man had offered me but *fivepence*, I would have taken it to get out of his shop! I was never able to go back to redeem my hat. I mended and re-mended my shoes, I mended my stockings, I bought my gloves from Armstrongs—from the sixpenny-box. They were never my size, or indeed, the same size; but that didn't matter for I never wore them, and a six-and-a-half and a seven carried perfectly well together.

On one memorable occasion, one of our number got a windfall—a prize for an essay competition sponsored by the church.

For weeks it had been part of my duty as senior student to report the disappearance of quantities of foolscap from the study. It did not dawn upon me that one of our number might be in the throes of literary aspiration—but we were greatly rewarded. The post-boy whistled at the front door, and five pounds arrived! Five pounds! And we spent most of it that very night—improvident or not—counting it all fun to wait for hours on cold steps, for the visiting opera company, that the whole House might enjoy the show.

Great days they were, with a passion for extracting from the unforgiving minute *just over* sixty seconds' worth of distance run! Added to our House lectures, we did club-leadership at the Y.W.C.A., psychology at the W.E.A., and occasional lectures at the 'varsity, at the public hospital, and at the sanatorium on the hills. We were each attached to a church, with leadership of a youth group, and week-day responsibilities among the poor. We ran jumble sales for those who attended our mothers' meetings, and wrestled as best we could in our virgin innocence with moral lapses and family instability. We might forget the date and might of the Diocletian persecution, but we dare not forget the number of teeth of Mrs. Brown's baby, or Mrs. Thompson's or Mrs. Jones's. Some of our more adventurous spirits did Saturday duty as working-witnesses at out-patients' department of the public hospital. Some went on to a full course at hospital, others to St. Helen's for midwifery. Those were usually girls preparing for overseas work. I went to Phillipstown Kindergarten, and to the Nurse Maud District Nursing Association. All the mornings of my second year I spent at the kindergarten. Afternoons found me in the wide spready city, bathing and brightening up the bedridden, dressing varicose ulcers, and giving injections.

Once a week I went to the dispensary, to toy with minute weights and a pestle and mortar, and help to fill up the huge ointment jars. I learned, if nothing else, how to behave in a sick-room—and early in my training, to lay out the dead for burial.

Day after day humanity poured in an endless stream through that dispensary: the sick, the distressed, the incompetent. Life had lent to Nurse Maud, the ageing founder of the Association, a pioneer spirit, and a pair of practical hands. Over the doorway hung a chaste plaque, bearing the words of Ambriose Paré, a surgeon of the sixteenth century: '*I nursed him*: *God healed him.*'

As my turn came, I went with another—and later, alone—to do police-duty at the public mortuary. The Association was called in always where the police were concerned, in cases of suicide, murder or accident.

My first call was to attend to the body of an old lady knocked down in the street. The bare facts I learned in the few minutes it took me to collect the key from the hospital hard by. Old Mrs. Dawson had been a favourite

71

and regular visitor at the hospital over the years—ever since her husband had died there.

The old lady's son had been grievously wounded in the 1914–18 war, and had been invalided home, sick in body and mind. In one of his 'turns' he had resisted his old mother, and had caused her to lose the sight of an eye. For years, Nurse said, she had been obliged to keep him away in an institution. Now the old lady had been knocked down in the street by a bicycle without a light, on her way to hospital for the evening visiting-hour.

The facts in themselves were a shock to me, as was my first grim duty at the mortuary, but together they were nothing like the shock that came to my spirit when my companion made reference to our unhappy task as 'the will of God'.

'The will of God!' The words struck me, and I had no words. The utterance had in it all the signs of blind resignation. And though I had not—being so young— thought it out, I felt sure there was something wrong about it. No wonder 'most people, when the will of God is mentioned, feel a cold shadow creeping over them'.

Was it the will of God that a man smitten with a hideous disease should die? That a son should be broken in body and mind? That an old lady, on her way to an act of kindness, should be knocked down by a larrikin on a bicycle, without a light? Could I make these things fit with God—*the God whom I had known through Jesus Christ?*

I could call the death of the father the result of a germ picked up in an unhealthy place of work; I could call it the follow-up of a constitution weakened by ignorance; I could call it a tragedy without a known cause—but I could not call it so glibly the will of God.

The son's sad lot I could call the harvest of war; or the result of faulty after-care—but not the will of God.

Old Mrs. Dawson's accident I could call an accident

plain and simple; I could call it the result of her impaired eyesight, or several other things—but I would not say it was the will of God.

It needed a lot of thinking about at twenty. Some words of an old hymn that I had heard sung many times, walked up and down in my mind:

> My God, my Father, while I stray
>   Far from my home, on life's rough way,
> O teach me from my heart to say,
>   'Thy will be done'.

And the next verse only reminded me of the unfortunate Mr. Dawson:

> Though pining sickness waste away
>   My life in premature decay,
> My Father, still I strive to say,
>   'Thy will be done'.

The next verse seemed to focus its sentiment on the poor, broken son:

> What though in lonely grief I sigh
>   For friends beloved, no longer nigh,
> Submissive still I would reply,
>   'Thy will be done'.

And the last verse refused to have any content but the tragic death of old Mrs. Dawson:

> Then when on earth I breathe no more
>   The prayer oft mixed with tears before,
> I'll sing upon a happier shore,
>   'Thy will be done'.

Whilst still I pondered these things, one of those curious coincidences occurred. That night I was called to a maternity home, as working-witness. It was questioned whether I ought to be allowed to go—I had had a long, taxing day. But in a few minutes I was on my bicycle and hastening over the half-mile to the home.

Sister met me at the door, efficiently thrust me into a theatre-gown, and showed me where I might scrub my hands.

And that night—a few minutes before midnight—a little new cry broke forth upon the world. The long planning of a home and the loving patience of two people had been realized. A little new life had come. *And no one spoke of it as 'the will of God'!*

My duty finished, I got into my coat, and pedalled home through the silent streets, my mind busy with the contrasting events of that day. I had been in the presence of Death—I had been in the presence of Life.

Sleep for me I confess did not come easily that night. My mind was busy.

People get comfort from feeling that their tragedies are the will of God, part of my mind said; say that death is an accident, a ghastly mistake, wilful stupidity or ignorance on the part of the individual, the family or society, and you have robbed the pious.

But is that comfort worth having, another part of my mind asked? Is there any final comfort in a lie? And it is a lie, to lay much of what happens at the feet of God, as being His will.

Certainly God can take the shattered parts of His purpose, after we have wrecked it, and make of them some goodly thing. It might be a new quality of courage, the lovely quality of kindness, or the tender service of sympathy—but one has no right to call all the tragedy and suffering that comes, the 'will of God'. The tragedy in the life of old Mrs. Dawson did not *make* courage and kindness —they were there all the time. Evil cannot create good, though sometimes circumstances resulting from evil, offer an opportunity for the expression of good. I saw it clearly.

It was not the will of God that brought the broken body of poor old Mrs. Dawson into our hands that morning. It was the sin of nations that broke the golden chalice of her boy's mind amid the barbed-wire and horrors of war; it was a breach of the by-laws of her own lovely city that broke at last her old body.

Certainly, it would have been unconventional to have spoken of the 'will of God' that same night when that little new life was given. But why? We have looked upon our Lord and have never related what we had seen to our everyday life. We have heard Him say a triumphant thing: 'My meat is to do the will of God, and to finish His work'—and again, like a battle-cry of joyous dedication: 'I seek not my own will, but the will of my Father which sent me.' And what was that will? Was it only Death? No! Said He: 'I am come that men might have life, and that men might have it more abundantly.' *Life! Spiritual life, physical, mental and social—a rich and balanced fulfilment— that was the will of God!*

So why, I argued, put 'Thy will be done!' over the last resting-place of our dead? Why not over the birthplace of our life—over our maternity-homes, and schools and churches and youth-clubs and playing-fields; why not over our homes, and libraries, and concert-halls and wireless-sessions; why not over our laboratories and hospitals where men and women probe Nature's secrets and combat disease? Ruskin said: 'People often pray this prayer, as if it were God's will to take away babies.' Why not learn to pray it joyously at the birth of babies?

The will of God, I saw clearly, had to do with every piece of honest truth—whether found in the discussion-group, the laboratory, the place of worship; with every live decision and action—whether in the place of pots and pans, ledgers and typewriters, or in the planning and scheming of the nation's leaders.

So I cast out the sentiment of the old hymn, and welcomed in its stead Mann's reinterpretation:

> *My God, my Father, make me strong,*
> *When tasks of life seem hard and long,*
> *To meet them with this triumph song,*
> *'Thy will be done!'*
>
> *Draw from my timid eyes the veil,*
> *To show, when earthly forces fail,*
> *Thy power and love must still prevail,*
> *'Thy will be done!'*

VIII

TOWARD the close of my second year I was appointed to preach—to take a share of services with the ministers, home missionaries and local-preachers. My appointments were mostly in wide country circuits where hard-pressed ministers were glad of some assistance, or in suburban churches, and appeared on the plans under the impersonal designation: 'Deaconess Student.' I liked going to the country.

I had exactly two sermons. One was a 'famous sermon'. I preached it everywhere. It was headed on my near manuscript: 'What is God Like?' My ignorance was vast—but so was my courage. I had just discovered that what Jesus was in *time*, that God is eternally—and I felt people ought to know that tremendous piece of truth at the earliest possible moment.

Philip's question, 'Show us the Father, and it sufficeth us', served me as text; and the moment of climax was reached with our Lord's words: 'He that hath seen Me hath seen the Father.' *So God was like Jesus!*

I traced with starry-eyed wonder the visions of men up through the long years. Isaiah had early discovered Him to be the God of Holiness. In his turn, Amos had said: 'Yes, but He is more—He is the God of Judgement.' And to his developing conception, Hosea had added: 'He is all you say—a God of Judgement, a God of Holiness—but He is more: a God of Mercy.' And so the answer stayed for many centuries, until at last came the revelation of Jesus: 'Yes,' said He, in effect, 'He is all the best that men have ever guessed of Him—but more: He is the seeking Father!' And when Philip put his question our Lord crowned that word with: '*He that hath seen Me hath seen the Father!*'

It was a wonderful revelation—and nineteen centuries later it was just as wonderful to me as it had been to those who heard it first. Dr. Nathaniel Micklem stated it well: 'In the hour when we awake to see that God is like Jesus, seeking our love and offering to us His love and His friendship through all life's story, and when we yield ourselves to love's demand, we thereby enter a new world, our spirits are come home to God our Saviour, and we are at leisure to pass on the reconciling word to others.' Never for one moment did it dawn upon me that my listeners might have heard it before. I couldn't think how they could remain the same people once they knew it. It made all the difference, as I saw it, to what one thought about the world in which one's life was set, with its far-reaching plains, and homes, and trees, and its 'pinch of star-dust, which is the Pleiades'; it made all the difference to what one felt about suffering and about sin. It said in effect:

In this vast universe
There is but one supreme truth:
That God is our Father.
By that truth meaning is given
To the remote stars, and the numberless centuries,
The long and heroic struggle of mankind.

O my soul, dare to trust this truth.
Dare to rest in God's kindly arms,
Dare to look confidently into His face,
Then launch thyself into life unafraid,
Knowing that thou art in Thy Father's house,
That thou art surrounded by His love.
Thou wilt then become master of fear,
Lord of life, conqueror even of Death.

So I preached—with the consent of all my faculties—so I lived!

At my valedictory service, one of the speakers said a memorable thing: 'When you leave this House,' said he, 'the value of this experience will lie, not in what you want to remember, *but in what you cannot forget.*' And so I found it.

Along with certain unforgettable experiences, were several unforgettable people—among them our Chaplain, and our Lady Superintendent, the Rev. W. J. and Mrs. Williams. They were gracious people; separately, and together, they had won wide distinction in the Church. Mr. Williams had been President of the Conference, preacher, Church historian, and Editor of the Connexional paper; he had served as Principal of Wesley College (Three Kings), and Secretary of the Board of Examiners. But perhaps we students will remember him best seated at the head of the long table, bowing his head in the blessing, or with a twinkle suggesting a topic for feminine conversation, or carving the joint for his large 'family', a little flustered, his snowy napkin tucked under his chin.

Mr. Williams's eldest son was already honoured beyond the bounds of Church and home, as one of New Zealand's most gifted sons. As a lad, he read Latin, Greek, Hebrew, French, Maori and Italian. He stood in even happier case than Thomas Manning, of whom Hine said: 'With his immense learning he could keep silent in fifteen languages.' Dr. Harold Williams read and spoke between forty and fifty—earning thus a unique place in international journalism. During the Great War, and the subsequent revolution, he served in Russia as official correspondent for *The Times*.

All my days in 'M.D.H.', I held Mr. and Mrs. Williams in reverent regard, but I was not 'out' long before our relationship developed into genuine and joyous friend-ship. It was good to find ourselves neighbours in a northern city, and to be able to lend each other books. One of the very last that Mr. Williams shared with me was an advance copy of the life of his gifted son, Harold, *Cheerful Giver*, written by his Russian wife, Ariadná Tyrkova Williams.

Our beloved 'Mrs. W. J. W.' had been a deaconess her-self before marriage. Snowy-haired, tall and dignified, it was a loss to us all when she moved to Melbourne, at Mr. Williams's death. Chief among my pleasures in that lovely city, a year or two ago, when I passed through on a lecture tour, was an opportunity to strengthen our friend-ship. She was among the little group that came down to the plane to meet me.

She showed undisguised pleasure in the fact that the Deaconess Committee had approached me with a view to my becoming Lady Superintendent of 'M.D.H.'. Un-happily, I was not able to accept that honour.

Mrs. Williams's letters, through the years, have been a rich and constant delight, displaying a grateful spirit, and a refreshing whimsicality.

Life gave me also in those student days of questing, a friend, Edna Lenna Button. A Tasmanian, 'Buttons' had already done six years of deaconess service in a great Melbourne mission. She came to 'M.D.H.' in my second year.

Life was big in 'Buttons'. She had the same love of Nature as my own—and though she was shy—a good deal more experience of human nature. Soon we were fast friends. We kept each other company on those cold morn-ings when we crept down to the study, before the House was astir; and in a dozen other escapades she brought to my life the stimulus of an eager personality. We spent the jolliest Saturday afternoons together, wet or fine, setting off on our 'bikes' till tea brought us home, with our arms full of selected sprays, or our handle-bars burdened with sprigs of flowering gorse. The fragrance of those things is with me still.

With a merry heart, she endeared herself to many—but I was her friend.

Guides, Cubs and Brownies loved her. Never waiting for votes of thanks, no job was beneath her dignity. Many a time they saw her prepare an appetizing meal out of next-to-nothing, coax old clothes into renewed life, half-sole shoes, prepare and lead a youth service, or with pen or crayons turn out posters that were alike the envy and delight of all who saw them. She was always making something. God lent her a valiant spirit, a good pair of hands, and a self-forgetfulness.

My first Christmas away from the fellowship of 'M.D.H.' she spent with me at Raetihi, and years later, when I was able to visit England, came north to do my job.

Soon after I returned, she resigned, and was herself in England for the breaking of the spring. She had set her heart on additional studies in one of the English colleges, but the coming of war in September broke in upon many student plans, her own included. She found herself lending a hand in the hurried evacuation of children from London, and later, in the uniform of a W.A.A.F. medical orderly.

'Death is inevitably associated with personal loss,' she once copied for me from something we loved, 'and the grief resulting from such loss is readily understandable—but why it should be necessary to parade and exploit such grief to an accompaniment of dingy black and dismal music, is beyond my comprehension. If music accompanies my passing, I would prefer Mendelssohn's "Spring Song" to Mendelssohn's "Funeral March".'

Her passing, alas, could not be accompanied by music; she was killed—one of the first—in the Battle of Britain.

But she is not dead. How could she be? For such valiant ones, life goes on. All thought of her is inevitably associated with the message of the 'Spring Song'— Life! 'May I wish you three hundred and sixty-five days of Life,' she once wrote to me for a birthday, 'this world holds nothing better.' She loved Life. The experience of it which has come to her now is happily no longer a matter of the counting of days. The ending of her last letter seems to ring from over the ramparts of the new life carrying a wider and larger meaning: 'Quite well—very well—and very much alive!'

> *I cannot think of Paradise a place*
> *Where men go to and fro,*
> *With harps of gold and robes that shame the snow.*
> *Better some simple task, a spirit free, to*
> *Act along the line of self-forget . . .*
> *To help God make a blossom or a star.*

She was my friend. Her lithe body, blasted by the hate of nations, lies with those others, 'the first of the few', in the famous burial-ground at Biggin Hill.

Alas, can we ring the bells backward?
Can we unlearn the arts that pretend to civilize and then burn up the world?
There is a match of science, but who shall beat the drums for its retreat?

IX

ONE sunny morning I picked up a telegram that lay on my desk. It said: 'Proceed at once to Raetihi Home Mission Station.' My heart raced.

Raetihi, for all I knew, might be a little palm-fringed island in the middle of the Pacific. Actually, it proved to be a small town in the middle of the King Country—to be approached by way of Ohakune Junction, in the middle of the night.

First, I must pack my few belongings, and set out for the North Island, by the all-night ferry.

I shared a cabin with three others, but except for the civilities, we never spoke. When the winds and furies of the Straits have a mind to, they can make this trip between the two islands an extremely unpleasant one. Once or twice I wakened and turned in the night, just long enough to say to myself: 'We're having a good trip.' The dull persistent engines chugged on.

By six next morning we were in port. It was a matter of getting dressed in relays, and feeling general satisfaction that it was over. The cabin was stuffy. A slopped-over cup of ship's tea and a not very crisp biscuit served as a hint: the stewards were anxious to get the luggage off.

With others I clambered up on deck. Above, the gulls wheeled. The air was full of their harsh, plaintive cries.

There was little need to hurry—I had time—lots of time, till three o'clock in the afternoon. In any case, the city was not properly awake—the milkmen were still rattling about their job exchanging full bottles for empties. The newsboys were still crying the early editions.

At three o'clock that same afternoon, with a great show of steam, the night express shook off friends and relations and pulled out of Wellington—facing the four hundred and twenty-six miles between Wellington and Auckland— *a journey of sixteen hours.*

The way, I soon discovered, lay over mountains and through tunnels. Gradually the weary hours wore on, daylight waned, and the cloak of night settled down. We rattled across viaducts and bridges—across wide and meandering streams, across rushing torrents, deeply-cut. And then it was quite dark—dark with a sinister mountain darkness. The lights dimmed, and clackety-clackety-clack of steel wheels on steel rails made monotonous music.

One part of my mind gave itself up to marvelling at the faith we placed in the man in the engine-cab. Then a grunt from someone turning in his uncomfortable seat brought my thoughts back to something nearer at hand. Then a guard entered, a signal-lamp all but covered in the crook of his arm. Cursing a little under his breath, he stepped over the outstretched leg of a sleeping passenger, and an awkwardly placed suit-case. The carriage door shut to with a dull click behind him, and the momentary racket of the swaying train was shut out once more into the night.

It was difficult to ignore the crick in one's back. Thought followed a line for a time, then came back inexplicably to its starting-place. One's past was all behind —one's future all to come. A yellow blur of a station light again and again flashed past, and there was with it, a momentary change in the song of the wheels.

At last I felt the monster steadying. Soon I was sure of it—it was pulling into Ohakune Junction—in the middle of the land, in the middle of the night. I turned quickly enough in my uncomfortable seat, rubbed the steam off the window-pane and looked out. There was nothing to be seen but a pinky-brown station, and a concrete platform. Under pools of light, guards and refreshment-room attendants were moving quickly and purposefully, with unbelievable reality.

Out of the strangers on the platform, one suddenly emerged and introduced himself as the steward of Raetihi Methodist Home Mission Station, muttered a welcome, and took my bags.

We headed away from the blurry lights and blinking people, wakened from various stages of sleep. My companion began a softly spoken running commentary along the nine miles of wiggly road, as we went, but it was all in darkness. In the crisp mountain air, the cowering mountain seemed only to make the darkness a deeper darkness. A rabbit flicked away in our headlights, hurrying with all speed into shelter of the roadside. After some time we swung down into little Raetihi, asleep—and up its broad main street, to the only house with a light at that hour.

The little town numbering in all a thousand souls, was going through the dispiriting experience of changing over from one way of life to another—from bush to farming. It had seen prosperous days, but now there were nineteen empty shops on the main street.

Added to that, a devastating bushfire had swept the country, till the townsfolk looked out on to a landscape resembling a Flanders battle-field. Many had taken shelter in stream-beds for days. When the danger had passed—and its passing had meant ruin for many—only gaunt blackened treetrunks remained. It was a depressing sight.

The number of folk at the little Methodist church had dwindled, and grown dispirited, many had moved away. Off and on there had been no Home Missionary to guide them.

By the end of the week they rallied to give me what they called 'a Welcome Social'.

We had the social, but I have never been quite so sure about the welcome. Early, the chairman up-rose and said: 'Well, we're very glad you've come . . . We thought we would have had a man. But I s'pose if we can't have a whole loaf, we can make the best we can *of half a loaf*'— which I thought rather a 'crusty' welcome.

In the town were few houses where there was any chance of getting a room. Some of the smaller ones were mill-houses, put up to serve a temporary need, some not even painted. The church owned a small house, but it was let to a woman and her children.

From door to door I went that December. Never before had I entered so fully into my Christmas text: 'There was no room for them in the inn.'

At weary last, I set up my few bits of things in a woman's onion room. The dry onion-shells were still on the floor when I entered, and I had to get down and gather them up. A tiny room off the veranda served me as study.

At the end of summer I moved to what promised to be better, and at the end of autumn moved again. I had discovered an empty cottage at the end of a blind road running up into the hills.

Weeds, it was true, and over-grown parsnips seeded almost to the top of its windowsills. Great tussocks of grass overlapped its steps. It was an ugly little place, a lean-to perched precariously, but it was to be 'home' to me, for a few shillings a week, and I was in the proper mood to appreciate it.

At one end it had a sizeable tank for rain-water, and a tap into the scullery. It had a good chimney and a rusty old black stove. Besides the windows at each end, there was a decent-sized one in front. True when first I saw it, it bore a burden of blue-bottle flies and cobwebs—but it looked down over the township, ten minutes away, and away off to the three great mountains, Ruapehu, Ngauruhoe, and Tongariro.

One of the urgent needs of a woman's heart is a place where she can be at peace, and set her things about her. This was my first adventure in home-making. I had a modest table and chair, a bed and a box of books. I remembered that when Bunyan married a wife as poor as himself, he said: 'This woman and I came together as poor as poor might be, not having so much household stuff as a dish or a spoon betwixt us both. But,' added he, 'she brought with her, good woman, something that was more precious to Bunyan than silver and gold: for in her modest bundle *were two books*.' I had happily more than two books. And I bought myself a couple of pots, and a pan, two cups and three plates and some cutlery. I added a coloured mat for my floor, I black-leaded my stove, and hung my curtains. Then I recalled my mother's words, 'Nothing so rewards a house-keeper as tidy curtains and a clean doorstep,' so I scrubbed my doorstep. And at the end of the day, limb-weary, I scrubbed myself.

Hungry, I set down my pan, and my couple of rashers of bacon. After a minute's silence, they began to splutter companionably. And so I turned my thoughts to the future with new courage.

But what would it be like I half asked myself, when darkness lay outside the windows, and an owl cried, 'a most melancholy cry shaken out long and clear upon the hill'? And what would it be like when rain fell, and the hilly clay path became all but impassable? What would it be like——? But I would not think so far ahead—to the nights when I would have to come alone to that little crooked gate among the hills.

I experienced soon enough all those dreads of homecoming. An owl in the willows, or an innocent frog flipping into the pond, served to make me latch the gate, and climb the hill quickly. I was never quite sure of myself approaching that frog-pond and clump of willows at night. I used to whistle to keep up my courage. Coleridge's words still have power to recall for me my emotions when I hurried to snick the latch:

> As one that on a lonely road
> Doth walk in fear and dread,
> And having once looked back, walks on
> And turns no more his head
> Because he knows a frightful fiend
> Doth just behind him tread.

One night I wakened suddenly with the sense of something unusual happening. My first thought was a light. I had then no experience in dealing with swaggers or mischief-makers. Ought I to concentrate on the poker, or offer kindly words? Whilst I was deliberating the knocking ceased. My watch told me it was two o'clock. The swagger, or whoever it was, likely got a scare, too, in finding the house inhabited.

Quiet restored, I put out the light, and lay in the velvety darkness, hearing the clock ticking—or was it my heart?

Next morning, when I went out, I related my experience to a friend. 'What you need,' said he, 'is one of my old coats, and a pair of my boots, in your porch.' I looked at him. 'Of course,' he continued, 'they're the very thing. Put them in your porch, and if anyone ever comes again, he'll think you have a man about the place.'

But I think I was never quite so brave again. Coming home at night, I fancy I started to whistle just a little bit farther up the road.

Money was hard to get. I lived for weeks, whilst I was

paying for my things, on a tin of honey, a brown loaf, and an overgrown plot of silver-beet that I'd inherited. I've never since been able, I confess, to look that succulent vegetable in the face.

For months I had no means of getting about save on my old push-bike. It had served me well on the flat streets of Christchurch, but it was not made for the pot-holes of the King Country in all weathers. For months, with occasional lifts from lorrymen, I managed, but as things gathered heart, there were more services, story-times, and clubs.

I thought about a horse—all Home Missionaries seemed to have been able to ride horses—but I'd only been on a horse once, to stay on—so I wasn't sure.

Then in a roundabout way I heard that the church owned a motor-bike. I didn't know anything about motor-bikes, except to argue that if a horse was quicker than a push-bike, a motor-bike would be quicker than a horse. But I have already told of that.

I went down to the garage-man to ask if it was true. Did the church own a motor-bike? 'Yes,' he said, 'it is true, in a sort of a way. They had a man here, and he rode it into the end of a bridge, and broke it up a bit, and broke his ankle and his collar-bone. But you can have a look at it. It's over there under that old cow-cover.'

So I had a look at it. I wasn't much impressed; but I opened its tool-box—the only thing I knew how to open and shut—and therein I found a little book of instructions, all about its innards. Not knowing what else to do, I took home the little book of instructions and straddled a chair in the kitchen, and learned it all off by heart—so that now I was doing this, and now I was doing that; now it was in this gear, and now it was in that.

And when I'd got the theory of it all into my head, I went off down to the garage-man, to ask if I might take out the motor-bike. 'Y-e-s,' said he, 'yes, of course. You're used to motor-bikes?' 'Well,' I was obliged to answer, 'I wouldn't exactly say I'm *used* to them—as a matter of fact, I've only been on a kitchen-chair so far.'

I am afraid he thought me a great fool. That hardly mattered, but if I was going to be a fool, then I liked to be it on my own. So I pushed the motor-bike out of sight of that man—and out of sight of any other man. Then I looked at it, and I was a little disconcerted to find that there were a lot of things in the book, that weren't on the bike. I saw that I'd have to spend some money on it. And I did: and by the mercy of Providence, and what things I had learned in the kitchen, I got it to go.

Next day I started it, rode it, stopped it and restarted and did everything I thought a motor-bike could do on the road. And that night—my services prepared—I brought it home to a friend's house, and held it panting away in the yard. An old neighbour looked over the wall, and asked me what I'd got. Well, I wasn't sure. He asked me what I was going to do with it: I knew that all right.

Then came a very heavy shower, a very heavy shower, as falls in that high country. 'Well, here's a shower to christen it anyway,' said he. 'What are you going to call it?'

I wasn't sure. 'Anyway,' I said, 'what do you call motor-bikes?' (About a month afterwards, I knew *several things* that I could have called it!)

'You ought to give it a name,' he persisted, 'ought to call it something. John Wesley, you know, rode a horse all over England, preaching and teaching.' But that didn't help us, for who ever heard of the name of John Wesley's horse? I suspect he wore out a good many—he rode so far and he rode so long—or was too busy ever to name them.

The rain was coming down increasingly hard. Not to be

outdone, my old friend offered another suggestion. 'Well, you'd better call it "John Wesley",' he said. And standing there I couldn't think of a good reason why we shouldn't—so we did.

In the days following, my people for miles around got to know the sound of the coming of 'John Wesley', and their Home Missionary. Let it be said to his credit, that he carried me hundreds of miles over those clay roads and ruts, and never once let me down, which can't be altogether dishonourable to the name of the great John!

For months on end, in the winter, I set out, Sundays and week days, in thigh gum-boots, with a haversack of dry things on my back. Countless times in those muddy miles, I squinted into blunt rain; countless times my gum-boots were shiny-black and dripping, my leather gloves sodden, my thighs without feeling, until I dismounted and whacked them. Then a sensation, as of thorns, came into them, and I wiped my eyes from which the wind had scooped tears as I rode. Countless times during those long exposed rides, I had to brace my arms, grip with my knees the pads on each side of the tank of my machine, and set my teeth. Sometimes snow fell. Sometimes there was sleet. In that high country winter was a stubborn siege.

I had no choice—I had to have something speedier than a push-bike—but I set it down as sober truth that motor-bikes are fit only for youths who want to break their necks, or someone else's. The only thing in their favour is that they are cheap—and at times they are the only way. Something a little more generous might be said for them on fine roads, in fine weather, but that was so seldom my lot.

Every Sunday morning and evening the year through I preached at the little main church. Before the morning service, I led the Sunday-school. After service I snatched a simple meal, and was eight miles off at another Sunday-school by two. At a quarter-to-three, I was speeding over the miles to take yet another service. So by the time I pronounced the benediction at the home-church at night, I was more than ready for my bed. I was the first woman in our Church to do this kind of work. *And I would have died rather than fail.*

On week-days I had, in addition to my study and pastoral visitation, two young people's clubs and two Guilds, and once a month I went by slow goods-train, miles off to a mill. That involved staying overnight. I went out in the early morning, visited the people—took a tiny Sunday-school, and taught and encouraged two of the mothers to keep it going till I came again. When the 'gong' went for the meal at the cook-house I took up my pannikin, and filed in with the men—and announced the meeting for the evening. They were men of few words—perhaps they were as shy of me, as I was shy of them.

If a certain mill-hand was at home, then I had to 'shake-down' or walk the miles back down the line to the Junction. So I made my visits as near as possible to the full moon. There was only one half of a double-bed to spare in that settlement.

I never minded my walks alone down the line, except when the dogs began to bark at the railway camp. A prison-camp lay a few miles distant, on the far side of the mountains, and I was always scared that the dogs would give rise to the belief that another prisoner had escaped. After the first scare I managed to slip by quietly, by taking off my shoes, and putting them on again half a mile on the other side. Somewhere between eleven and midnight, I would find a front-door key under a mat at Ohakune.

One of our veteran Home Missionaries, the Rev. Christian Aker, enjoyed to tell how he visited my folk,

WONDER-LUST
(Early Spring)

and I took him to a mill service by goods-train. We lugged into the camp a magic-lantern, and a haversack of slides and hymn-books.

At night, when the service was over, I bade him good-night. 'You'll be all right,' I said, 'I hope you'll have a comfortable night. I'll meet you in the morning at the Ohakune Junction.

In the morning Mr. Aker's old weathered face carried an added smile. After preliminary remarks, he said: 'Dear goodness, do you know where they put me to sleep last night? On an awful old couch made into something of a bunk in a corner of the cook-house; and it had one or two slats missing in a vital spot. I couldn't get to bed till all the men had cleared out, and I had to be up this morning at half-past four, when the man came to stoke up. I had an awful night,' he added, 'the old thing wasn't long enough, and when I got my shoulders arranged, my feet were out, and when I got my feet in, my shoulders were out.' (Mr. Aker was over six foot). 'How do you manage?' he asked quizzically. 'What do you do when you go there?' 'Just what you did last night,' I replied, 'only I'm not so jolly tall as you.' 'And how did you get on last night?' asked he. 'Very well—I walked into the Junction—eleven miles,' said I, '*to give you the only bed, since you were our guest!*'

So I managed to wrestle with long distances and loneliness, building my Bethels out of stony griefs. Some great stories—family stories—I shared, but they were the kind of stories I have never told, and will never be able to tell.

Of course, it was not all work. Now and again there were days when I gave myself up to the earth-scents and the sky-winds and all the magic of the countryside which is ordained for the healing of the soul.

And there was the unforgettable day when I got my *Encyclopædia*—ten sturdy volumes in red. Lots of things

SC—D

might be disappointing, but I had those volumes. I carried them into the little vestry, on my way from the post, to have a private gloat over them. I could have taken them home, but that would have meant another fifteen minutes—*and I couldn't wait!*

It was a high privilege to minister to those widely-scattered folk. The great events of birth, death and marriage drew us very close together. And three times in as many months, with hard-working families, I looked into the face of tragedy—never an easy thing when financial failure, guns and water-holes are concerned.

At first, I had no authority of Church or State to conduct the service of marriage, and we had to save up our weddings till we could have two or three on the one day, and get a minister from the next circuit forty miles away, or the Chairman, distant a day and a night's journey.

When the Church Conference met it voted that I should have full authority. Only afterwards was it discovered that a law of the land used the term 'male agent of the Church'. No one had had occasion to notice the word 'male' before, and we had to be content to wait until the innocent word could be erased by the slow wheels of Parliamentary procedure.

The most embarrassing service of worship I ever led was at Raetihi. We had had some special services, when one morning I met the mayor of the town—who was also the cabinet-maker, the undertaker, and the superintendent of the Fire Brigade. 'Could we have a Church-parade for the men?' he asked. I thought we could; and I passed on the date to the choir. They got up a special anthem; and I got up a sermon on 'Peter, beside the fire of coals!'

The chosen Sunday evening came and there was a goodly congregation. The firemen filed in, during the voluntary, making a striking picture in their smart uniforms, and carrying their great brass helmets. They seated themselves, and clonked their great helmets under the seats.

It was an impressive service. According to custom, we had the call to worship, the hymn, prayer, notices, the offering, and anthem, and were getting on nicely with Peter—when the fire-bell rang! In an instant, all the men picked up their helmets and ran out, and a goodly number of the congregation with them. The faithful 'regulars' looked up at me appealingly, cast between common consideration, and an urgent desire to know whose house was burning down.

I saw it was hopeless to continue with Peter. So as best I could, I came to a close, and pronounced the Benediction—and we had the last hymn the next Sunday.

It was a great blaze, though nothing like the damage was done that must have resulted, had not the volunteer brigade been all in one place, of one mind, at the one moment.

For myself, I like to remember that at least *once* folk were so anxious to get down to work that they were unable to hear me out!

X

NEVER for one moment did I doubt the validity of my call to preach, nor had I reason to believe that those who worshipped with me did either. I remembered that to a woman was entrusted the news of the Resurrection, upon which the very Church was founded. To Mary, in the Easter Garden, was given the words of our Risen Lord: 'Go tell My brethren . . .!' Nothing, I knew, could ever detract from the significance and honour of that great moment.

All through His ministry our Lord had regarded equally men and women. It was difficult to realize how revolutionary that was. Doubtless, He heard often in the synagogue, the morning prayer upraised to 'Bless God who has not made me a Gentile . . . a slave . . . or a woman.' The position of women even in the proud Roman Empire was one of inferiority. The attitude of our Lord, on that account, was the more striking. It was true, He did sometimes speak to His men and women hearers alternately, but His story of the coin lost in the house, followed hard on His story of the sheep lost out in the hills; He drew as clearly the word-picture of the housewife examining her rugs for moths, as the picture of the craftsman looking over his tools for the first signs of corroding rust. And His healing power was extended as graciously to each: so that on one occasion He healed an epileptic boy, beloved of his father, and on another occasion drew from the gates of Death, a little girl of twelve; once on a Sabbath day within the synagogue, He healed a man with a withered hand, and on another, an elderly, bowed and bent woman; once, *in absentia*, He extended His healing to a Roman centurion's servant, and on another occasion, to the daughter of a Gentile woman of Syrophoenicia.

That no woman was chosen among the Twelve, was obviously a matter of local propriety, and not one of principle. For that matter, the Twelve were all Jews, though Churchmen who argued the validity of the 'apostolic succession', in no way limited it to Jews. Women were not partakers of the first Lord's Supper, yet no one had suggested that they should be excluded on that account. They were present on the day of Pentecost, when the Early Church experienced the out-pouring of the Holy Spirit.

Only those, it seemed, who made exceptions where they suited, took the Scriptures literally, or forgot for the moment the time and social setting of the Early Church, found any difficulty in Paul's injunction to the women to 'keep silence in the Churches'. Unlike the men, many of them were but little educated—as in parts of the East to-day—and when the apostle's exhortation went on for hours, as it often did, they found it quite impossible to follow, or irksome, to say the least of it. So they turned to other things. The word Paul used meant literally 'conversation carried on in an undertone'—what we would call 'soft chatter'. Where they showed a real desire to learn, and wanted further help, Paul added: '*Let them ask their husbands at home, for,*' said he, '*it is a shame for women to speak in the church.*'

In this instance, as in so many, Paul's injunction was plainly spoken to meet a particular situation, and was not meant to be accepted as a binding principle. Above all, stood out his constant tribute to 'those women which laboured' with Him in the Gospel, and his glorious summing-up: 'There is neither Jew nor Greek'—*racial discrimination*—'there is neither bond nor free'—*social dis-*

crimination—'there is neither male nor female'—*sex discrimination*—'for all ye are one in Christ Jesus.'

After a time I was transferred to Otorohanga, a growing town in the pastoral Waikato. I had now finished my probationary period as a member of the Deaconess Order, and been publicly dedicated—and set apart for special work.

Otorohanga hitherto had been served by a Home Missionary from afar. With my appointment the people were to have for the first time a Home Missionary of their own.

In a number of ways the pattern of my days was much as at Raetihi, even to the difficulties of accommodation and transport. And the same winds of economy blew about my little house. The people, however, welcomed me cordially.

They soon realized that I would need some way of getting about. But they hadn't much money, and they hadn't many ideas; so they did a thing that people do when they have little money and few ideas—*they had a meeting*. It was a men's meeting—I was the only woman there. They were fine farming men, but not eloquent at church meetings, and about five minutes to eleven, one of their number got up and said 'Well, I haven't had my say yet. I don't know exactly what we're going to do, but I understand that our new Home Missionary can ride a motor-bike. I've got an old motor-bike in the back of the hay-shed—and look, I'll give it to her.' The next words I heard were those of the chairman: 'If the gentlemen will rise, we will now have the benediction.' So we had it.

And by eleven o'clock we'd had everything there was to have, and I'd got another motor-bike I didn't want.

I got it out of the hay-shed—it was a crazy old thing, but I pulled it to bits, and put it together again, and sold it to a Maori man for six pounds, in broad daylight. It wasn't a bargain, either. And with the six pounds I bought another, and pulled that to bits and put it together again —and christened it 'Charles Wesley', the brother of John. But when I recalled that there were *nineteen* in the Wesley family, I began to be a bit discouraged.

I journeyed thousands of miles on that old motor-bike. When the sticky clay roads in the hilly country put up too big a handicap, I left it with clogged wheels on the road-side, and tramped on.

One of the obstacles in the way of country-people and townspeople understanding each other, is that towns-people so seldom go into the country on a wet day. I did a lot of visiting on wet days. Though costly in effort, I found it most rewarding—on those days the whole family was indoors.

Most mornings in towns the sun has been up an hour or two before the head of the house opens his door and stretches out a pyjamaed arm to take in the milk-bottle and the morning paper. How can he expect to understand his brother, turned out of bed before the stars have gone in, his feet thrust into heavy boots weighted with mud, seeking out in the grey unfriendliness of the dawn, forty or sixty cows that must be milked, before he can get his share of milk and the morning paper?

Many towns-folk still cling to the idea that living in the country differs hardly from living in the town, save that you look out on to green fields and farm buildings, in-stead of busy streets and shops, and listen to birds whistling instead of errand-boys.

That, of course, is hardly the truth. Folk who live in the country have a different type of mind, and a different set of problems. They do not as a rule easily tell their thoughts; they spend many more hours alone; they are almost all of them practical. Of course, they have their

99

own funny little ways—a strong aversion, for instance, to using their front doors and front rooms. They spend a good deal more time in their homes; they have less organized entertainment; they ponder more profoundly the things that catch their interest, and loyalties, once gained, go deep.

Around the earth, one of every two men gainfully employed is a farmer. He may be scratching over a strip of soil in India, raising barely enough to keep his family alive; he may be using the most up-to-date method of conserving his pasture-lands in our own little country, or gathering in the waving gold on the corn-fields of Canada. Whether he tills the ancestral acres, or breaks new country, he deals constantly with the processes of life—birth, reproduction, death; the impersonal forces of nature—the seasonal rainfall, shifting temperature, insects. *He thinks in terms of the continuity of life.*

Does farming pay? Some say Yes, and some say No. Is farming an agreeable life? Again, some say Yes, and some say No. But if the land fails. . .? William Langland asked that question away back in 1362, in *The Vision of William concerning Piers the Plowman*, and his answer is still the answer we must give:

> *If the land fails?*
> *Then fails meat and bread, for both rich and poor,*
> *And all manner of men that by meat and drink labour.*
> *Therefore, let all manner of men who by meat live,*
> *Help him to work vigorously who winneth our food.*

Farming is not a task for the faint-hearted. Countless times I crossed the lush paddocks, with the cows lying in the sun, lethargic, eternally chewing, but I knew that such prosperity had been hardly won. Hard work, and a wholesome respect for it, was as a bond between us, as I moved amongst my people.

In addition to the farmers and their families whom I served were the towns-folk—the doctor and his wife, the grocer, the matron of the hospital, the hardware merchant, the garage-man.

Again and again in our worship some heavenly 'over-plus' was added; again and again young folk joined the Church; again and again, by the grace of God, some quiet soul found that he could lay down his burden and take away a strength that made him other than he was.

There were always folk, of course, who never came to church. It was always the weather or the distance or something. As Principal Macgregor used to say: 'It takes an extraordinary concatenation of meteorological circumstances (every syllable of every word lovingly and lengthily pronounced) to make it possible for some people to come to Church.'

I did not try to do a man's job—but I tried very hard to do my own. If ever I forgot the shining truth of the Poet Laureate's words it was not for long:

For woman is not undeveloped man,
But diverse: could we make her as a man,
Sweet love were slain: his dearest bond in this,
Not like to like, but like in difference.
Yet in the long years, must they liker grow.
The man be more of woman, she of man.
He gain in sweetness and in moral height,
Nor lose the wrestling thews that throw the world.
She mental breadth, nor fail in childward care,
Nor lose the childlike in the larger mind.
Till at the last she sets herself to man
Like perfect music unto noble words.

At my last country Synod, the Chairman, Percy Paris, of loved memory, invited me to preach at St. Paul's. Never had I faced so many clerical collars. Beyond the text, I do not now remember what I said, but I shall remember always what someone else said. When I had finished, a minister uprose to express the thanks of the company. He stood a moment in silence, then he said this lovely thing that might rejoice the heart of any preacher: '*I came to this place to see Jesus more freshly and thank you, I have seen Him.*'

XI

In the early nineteen-thirties—in what are now known as 'the depression years'—I was moved north, 'midst the crowd, the hum, the shock of men.' I hated leaving the country; my work there was full of promise. But our largest city, like many another, had queues waiting. Strong men out of work walked the streets; youths and girls, ready for their life-work, perhaps suffered most—even casual gestures bespoke an apathy quite foreign to normal, happy workers. And the truth of the social gospel hammered at our hearts: 'Any present-day theology which has not a revolutionary sociology as part of its implicit logic is not truly Christian.'

Pain and tragedy were our constant companions in that Central Mission—and human stupidity. One of the most difficult things in the world, I soon learned, was to lift the spirit, and quicken the will, when the body was hungry or undisciplined; and like unto it was the difficulty of giving *things* to people, the new poor, without injuring their pride and self-respect.

That was one reason why I hated jumble-sales, though there seemed no way of managing without them. Sometimes, of course, they did take on a lighter turn. Tragedy and comedy were so intermingled in those days that it was difficult to tell where one ended and the other began; but always I felt those weekly jumble sales would be the death of me.

On one occasion Richard Arthur's furniture mart sent us a tomb-stone—a perfectly good tombstone. Its only inscription read: 'Here lies the body of a British hero. Amen.' I wondered what to do with it. Then a wit

among my helpers suggested that we 'ought to hang on
to it for a while—after all,' said he, '*we could easily add
"ine" on to the end of Hero.*'

To me, Fred Kitchen's poem still strikes a poignant
note, for all its flippancy:

> *Come and bewail the bedraggled tale*
> *Of bargains bought at the jumble sale.*
> *Reefer-coat and swallow-tail,*
> *Brought before the judgement rail.*
> *Never-ending sounds of rending:*
> *Trousers past the age of bending:*
> *Much-worn suits the eye offending:*
> *Anything one cares to send in. . . .*
> *Eager faces matching laces:*
> *Shoes too small, and broken braces:*
> *Ornaments for empty spaces . . .*

And there were a number of other features of work and
staffing in that Mission as painful to me as those jumble
sales.

I spent days and nights interviewing folk, one by one,
who came for a patient listener, a meal-ticket or an old
coat. I heard stories so sordid and grim that there dried
up in me for ever any desire to read murder stories and
thrillers. Hours I spent on the 'phone, trying to comb out
imposters; hours at night half-soling shoes, and planning
and preparing work for sewing-guilds. As time passed,
and the task assumed frightening proportions, Civic and
Mission organizations banded together to operate from
a central office.

On the spiritual side—though there was never any real
way of dividing the day's responsibilities into 'secular' and
'sacred'—I preached once every Sunday, led the Sunday-
school, young people's discussion group, took my place in
the adult choir, and guided the affairs of the children's

choir. During the week I tried to stretch my skimpy garment of time and energy over the young people's club, the mothers' meeting, some court work, prison visiting, and a share in the financial burden of the work. I managed also a weekly broadcast from one of the city studios, and the guidance of a children's library.

The library, like much that put up a challenge to me, was a legacy from the past. It was over-burdened with books, I found, dingy in the extreme, and completely out-of-date.

At one time an earnest librarian had been so careful to preserve the morals of his young readers, that he had gone through the library book by book, and scored out with a heavy pencil all such words as 'damn', 'blast', 'sneer'. Blasphemy and suggestive language that spread itself beyond single words, had proved a little more difficult to deal with; a lot could be covered by the words 'drunken oaths'. Death-bed scenes had not bothered him, and no flabby theme, it seemed, had been rejected, provided it was tied together with a so-called evangelical sentiment. Whether the books proved enjoyable to their young readers had been scarcely a matter for consideration: they were not there to be enjoyed—they were there to do them good. But the children I knew, had long outgrown that idea. The boys used to hold the pages of the books up to the light, *to see what words were under the pencil-scratchings*.

Agnes Repplier tells of another who 'found something to erase in all her children's books'; and Miss Edgeworth, of an earlier generation, described with grave complacency, a pathetic little library, scored, blotted, and mutilated. The volumes, she admitted, were hopelessly disfigured; 'but shall the education of a family be sacrificed to the beauty of a page? Few books,' added this responsible one, 'can safely be given to children without the previous use of the pen, the pencil, and the scissors. These, in their corrected state, have sometimes a few words erased, sometimes half a page.'

The Mothers' Meeting was another odd legacy. I could never quite see why it was called 'the Mothers' Meeting', since a goodly number of the members were single women; and when I had won their confidence, I tried to change its name to Women's Fellowship; but I do not flatter myelf that I changed its nature very much. Some fine women were members of that meeting, but a few were characters.

There was dear old Mrs. G——, who wanted to wear a golden crown.

Appalled by some of the words they sang, I tried to raise the standard of their choice. I tried to point out that one ought not to sing things one didn't believe—it wasn't honest. I suggested that a swinging tune wasn't the only thing. I quoted Dr. Maud Royden as saying that if a thing was too silly to say, one could set it to music, and people would sing it.

At the end of a month or two, I felt the results were rather encouraging. I should have known better. At the very next meeting when the opening hymn was called, it was:

> *I shall wear a golden crown*
> *When I get Home:*
> *I shall lay my burdens down,*
> *When I get Home.*

Tactfully—without even waiting to hear the tune—I suggested that this was one of those hymns that we had been talking about. I went on to elaborate.

When the Scripture writer, an Easterner, upon whose words this hymn was based, I said, sat down to write what he believed about the life beyond, he soon found himself struggling with the limitations of language. So he adopted a rich imagery for that most glorious existence—streets of gold, and gates of pearl.

Centuries later, when the hymn-writer—a Westerner, and far more literal—came upon his words, he took them very much at face value, and many ever since have gone on singing them in that same literal sense.

I was treading on dangerous ground, I knew, but I thought we were getting on nicely. My satisfaction alas, was short-lived, for the moment I ceased speaking, there arose from old Mrs. G—— a cry that sounded like nothing so much as the cry of a lost soul: 'Oh, Sister—*I wanted to wear a golden crown!*'

For a moment, I was at a loss for a word. Then it struck me as being rather humorous, for as long as I had known old Mrs. G—— she had worn a man's black felt hat with the top punched out, and I couldn't help thinking, Well, if that's your idea of Heaven—to get away from that wretched old black felt hat, then I don't blame you altogether. But it was no subject for humour, and what I said was something rather different.

'A golden crown!' It had surprised me that anyone could really want to wear a golden crown; but then I was young, and had no old black felt hat. There were conceptions of the Here-after that meant much more to me than that; I liked the idea behind the text: 'His servants shall serve Him.'

On second thoughts, I knew it was not only my youth, for somewhere I had come upon a poem by an old lady, quite as old as Mrs. G——:

> *I pray that risen from the dead*
> *I may in Glory stand——*
> *A crown—perhaps—upon my head,*
> *But a needle in my hand.*

107

I never learned to sing or play,
So let no harp be mine,
From birth until my dying day,
Plain sewing's been my line.

Therefore, accustomed to the end
In plying useful stitches,
I'll be content if asked to mend
The little angels' breeches.

Another character in those days was old Mrs. 'Oward. Mrs. Howard had six letters to her surname though for all practical purposes, five did just as well. She loved to come early to 'the Meeting', to sit with a sprinkling of early-comers, to await my arrival, her face wreathed with smiles.

Mrs. 'Oward lived in Hobson Street—in a bed-sitting-room. Her husband, Willy 'Oward, had died long before I knew her. I was often in her strangely jumbled bed-sitting-room. A shiny press photograph of Willy and his comrades in music, taken at a band contest, held pride of place on Mrs. 'Oward's little crowded mantelshelf. Willy, short and round, had played the cornet, and from repeated accounts of that feat, had 'played it somethin' luv'ly'. I never heard what else Willy did.

For some years when I knew her Mrs. 'Oward had lived alone. Mothers' Meetings were life's big events. She wasn't a mother, but that didn't matter; she was a home-keeper, or had been, a bit hard-up, and at times lonely—or at least, she would have been 'if it hadn't been for the meetin's'. The plain truth was Mrs. 'Oward 'took to' Mothers' Meetings, like some people take to bridge, golf, committees, or the raising of prize blooms. It was a little vice she had that did nobody any harm. Having no kith or kin it was dull sitting alone, even with Willy up there on the mantelshelf, playing his cornet 'somethin' luv'ly'.

On Monday, wet or fine, Mrs. 'Oward was required by her own unyielding programme, to be at St. Matthew's at two. The meetin' there, and also the person in charge of it, was 'somethin' luv'ly'. On Tuesday she was at St. Mark's, Wednesday was Mrs. 'Enderson's, Friday was divided between 'the fortnightly' at St. Peter's, and 'the fortnightly' somewhere else. Thursday brought Mrs. 'Oward to us. So life was full of colour, from the time she slammed the door on Willy and the cornet, till she got home again—full also, of course, of community singing and cups of tea. 'A real good sing do warm yer up,' many a time I've heard Mrs. 'Oward say; the tea she consumed without comment—Mrs. 'Oward was too much of a lady for that. Everybody knew Mrs. 'Oward's love for 'two good cups of strong'.

On the particular day I have in memory, it was 'ours'—Thursday, and Mrs. 'Oward had arrived early as usual. Next moment, that thin face wreathed with smiles was approaching me. 'Sister,' she began, 'I've 'ad a wonderful answer to prayer.'

'Good!' I said. 'Tell me about it.'

Fully launched, Mrs. 'Oward began.

'Well, it was like this. Tuesday, I was sittin' up in Mrs. 'Enderson's meetin'. An' there I was prayin' ter Gawd, and prayin' ter Gawd when all of a sudden I remembered. I'd left me 'lectric iron on.' She paused for breath. 'An' there I was prayin' ter Gawd, and prayin' ter Gawd as 'E'd shut up Mrs. 'Enderson, so as I could go 'ome and turn it off. And d'you know, she shut up shorter'n she'd ever shut up before, and I went 'ome'—this with great solemnity—'*an' only the top of the safe was burnt.*'

'Well,' I said, 'that was wonderful.' And to give myself time to think, I repeated it, 'T-h-a-t w-a-s w-o-n-d-e-r-f-u-l.' I did not smile—it was a far too serious matter.

It may have needed the intervention of the Almighty to

'shut up Mrs. 'Enderson'—but why didn't it occur to Mrs. 'Oward that the same Almighty one, Maker of heaven and earth, had given her a little sense, and that it might have been a great deal more pleasing to Him if she had used it, and gone home at once and turned off her electric-iron?

But no, the proper purpose and province of prayer had never occurred to poor old Mrs. 'Oward; she'd had a wonderful answer to prayer, and my rational suggestion looked like throwing cold water in the face of the Almighty.

XII

In the midst of his full life John Oxenham paused to thank God 'for the things that seemed not good, yet turned to good'. And I have had to do that.

When I was at Raetihi, 'Buttons' travelled north to spend Christmas with me. But soon a telegram arrived to say that a beloved uncle was ill, and that if she wanted to see him she ought to hasten. It was disappointing, but 'Buttons' left at once to join her auntie and cousin.

And in the hours of their special need, and after her uncle's passing, she was so good to them that they were at a loss to know what to do for her. They made her a gift and contrived a brief holiday, but in no way felt they had discharged their indebtedness.

Often she spoke of her friend 'Snowie' at Raetihi, and later when she was due in Auckland for the annual Church Conference, it seemed an excellent chance for them to be together.

So God gave to the three of us—Rene, 'Buttons', and myself—that richest thing of all the years, our wonderful friendship.

In the *Testament of Friendship* Vera Brittain draws attention to the odd fact that from 'the days of Homer, the friendships of men have enjoyed glory and acclamation, but the friendships of women, in spite of Ruth and Naomi, have usually been not merely unsung, but mocked, belittled, and falsely interpreted'. Vera Brittain's *Testament* —the story of her glorious friendship with Winifred Holtby—has been claimed as the first real contribution of its kind to our literature. It seems odd that this should be so.

At first, our friendship had to be strengthened mostly by correspondence, but when I came to my work in the city, and to Rene's home, and later still, when 'Buttons' joined me in that work, it became the strong gift that it was—an adventure of mind and spirit that never for one day knew jealousy or distrust. Some day, out of our experience, I mean to write another *Testament of Friendship*.

One holiday time Rene and I turned our thoughts and plans toward the Milford Track, 'the loveliest walk in the world'. We got ourselves each a haversack, and a stout pair of shoes, and meant to meet in the south. We planned with great eagerness our introduction to the mighty peaks, streams, and bush tracks.

But first, Rene had to attend a youth conference; my days meanwhile were to be full of the 'strenuous joys' of running a health camp for mothers and children.

Then quite suddenly, one summer morning it was at an end. The carrier was due—the campers waited with bags and bundles. Just to make sure that all windows and doors were safely snicked, I ran back through the two houses we had used—and tripped and sprained an ankle.

As I was helped on to the carrier's lorry, clearly before my eyes rose our plans for Milford. Back in the hostel where I lived, somebody climbed to the third floor and packed for me. And a little doubtfully, I set off on my long journey south, stick in hand.

Three days and nights later I joined Rene at a southern railway junction. Her first exclamation was to compliment me on my good sense in bringing a stick; but soon the dispiriting truth dawned upon her.

In these early camp days at Queenstown we did all we could to prepare me for the track—but it was hopeless.

'What you need, of course,' said the camp nurse, 'is a good bandage. We'll get one.'

'What you need,' said another, as time passed and my disappointment deepened, 'is to put your ankle into hot salt water.' And two friends borrowed the vicar's copper, and dragged it over to the parish hall, where we were camping on straw. But it was of no avail.

'A liniment, well rubbed in, is what you want,' said someone else.

'The only really effective thing for a sprain of this sort,' said yet another, 'is to put your foot under running water.' And I hobbled to a little waterfall that splashed down conveniently near the road. But it was no use. The Milford Track—six strenuous days of streams, trees and mountains—was as far away as ever.

As our friends left, Rene and I were scarcely in the mood to echo Oxenham's *Te Deum*. We stayed on in peaceful Queenstown, within sight of the mighty ranging Remarkables, mirrored in the Lake, changing a thousand times a day. And as the days passed something we needed came through the strength and grandeur of those mountains.

We could not know it, but for what lay ahead we needed not the strenuous Milford Track, but that quiet, restful holiday. So 'again the thing that seemed not good, was turned to good'.

On our return north and to Rene's home, I sought out a doctor. 'What you need,' said he, 'is to put your feet up for two weeks.'

'But I can't possibly do that,' I replied, 'I'm too busy.'

Little did I know that within a few days I would have put them up for *two years*!

One of the lessons that must be learned sometime I suppose, is that no one is as important to the purposes of the day as she thinks she is; and another is that we are all 'bound up together in the bundle of life.' *Unearned good* comes, but the counter-law is just as operative—bringing *unearned ill*, through the selfishness, ignorance or stupidity of others. During the years to come I was to muse often on that law—and on the fairness of it—to save my spirit from bitterness.

In the Mission I had inherited a disused class-room, full almost to the ceiling with old clothes. They had been gathered to give away, but on examination had been seen to be quite impossible. So they had been thrown into the class-room to get them out of the way. Gradually over the years they had been allowed to accumulate, until with the rain dripping through a faulty roof, they had become an unpleasant mildewy mass, all but blocking up the window.

I knew I ought to do something about them. St. John's provided me with a strong fumigant, and I sealed up the room. Then with several good helpers, I set about the task.

But I developed a heavy cold, and had to retire. At the end of a week, the doctor found me in bed.

'Where have you been?' he asked. And the story of the old clothes room came out. But what had that to do with a heavy cold? Or was it pleurisy?

'You have collected a germ on the lining of your heart,' said he—giving it an impressive name. 'I want you to stay in bed—still, perfectly still—quite flat—no moving about—and I'll come to-morrow.'

He came on the morrow, and again on the morrow. Then he took Rene aside. 'This is going to be a long job,' said he. 'How are you placed? Are you here alone?'

'Yes,' answered Rene, 'but I can nurse her. We are here alone. She has just come to live here. I am a teacher of music, busy till late each evening: I'm also housekeeper— Mother is away: and I'm Dominion Secretary of the Presbyterian youth movement—but we'll manage somehow.'

And we did. How Rene matched the many needs of those weeks and months that spun into years, is still a matter for wonder.

Disquieting symptoms began to show. And by degrees another legacy of irresponsibility came to light.

During my Home Mission days I had needed a dentist, and at the suggestion of some good friends had sought out a surgery in an adjoining town that I might accept their hospitality at the day's end.

Though I had been struck by the dentist's manner when I made known my need, I had thought nothing of it, but when I came round from the anæsthetic, I said: 'There's something flipping about in my mouth.' 'So there is,' said he, 'I'll snip it off.' It proved to be a piece of the under-surface of my tongue. I went home to my friends, and it hæmorrhaged and swelled. When the news got around the district, it was as a joke that the dentist had taken a *bit off the woman-preacher's tongue*. And many got to know of it, because a little new church was due to be opened, and I could not attend.

The trouble to all appearances, cleared up and I might have thought nothing more of it, except that one night as I travelled on the late train, a woman spoke to me. 'You are Miss Rita Snowden, aren't you?' she asked. 'Did your tongue ever get right that time?'

With a twinkle, I replied: 'Oh yes—at any rate, my friends think it is *perfectly* all right.'

'You won't know me,' she continued, 'but I'm the wife of the dentist who did that for you. My husband was awfully worried about it. You see it was a race day, and he'd been racing his horses—and hadn't been winning. And I'm afraid he'd been drowning his sorrows.'

'I thought his behaviour a little odd,' I added, 'but if I had known the cause of it, he would have had *more sorrows to drown*. No one has a right to put another under an anæsthetic when he can't see what he is doing. He could have put me off till the morrow, or given me any excuse.'

'He has given up the work now,' added his wife lamely, and I learned that official action had been taken on other counts.

As I lay month after month waging my battle for health, the mischief of the thing manifested itself. A little suppurating point appeared on my gum, where I had sur-rendered a tooth those years before.

'We will have to call in your dentist,' said my doctor.

His examination made, the dentist said : 'I will have to get my nurse down.' And with my doctor's permission, they propped me up in my study chair. But it was of no use.

'Lie down for three weeks,' said my doctor, 'and we will take you in to have an X-ray.'

The X-ray revealed a fang of tooth, suppurating in my gum, the work of that slightly muddled dentist.

'Rest for a few more weeks,' said the doctor, 'and we will get the dentist and nurse down again.'

Though they were able to rid me of the offending fang, my jaw was affected ; and the nurse came day after day to dress it. So the wretched business dragged on and months passed.

'I think we will get you to a specialist,' said my doctor. 'But first lie quiet for a few weeks, and get your pulse down.'

Only those who have sojourned in the dark places of weakness and depression can know what these things mean : let others thank God if this outline of a battle is incomprehensible.

'Open your mouth,' said the specialist. 'Ah, septic tonsils—from that old fang. Go home and rest, and we will take you into hospital.'

Early in the evening before I was due to leave for

hospital, a long-distance telephone call came to say that my mother had had a stroke—could I come to Nelson? No. I couldn't so much as answer the telephone. And whilst we wondered, a second call came to say that she had gone.

So I went to hospital.

And returned.

I learned much about life in those years—and also much about sick-visitors. So often I listened to the same opening sentence: 'Oh, you p-o-o-r dear, *why should this have happened to you*?' I hadn't the strength to argue. Why should it *not* have happened to me? The inference of course was that since I was Christian, and doing what seemed a useful Christian job, I should somehow have been exempt from the results of human carelessness, and germs. Leaving out of account the good, kind hearts of my visitors—and I never for a moment doubted them—it seemed altogether very muddle-headed; as muddle-headed as the old idea that all suffering was the result of sin.

The fact of suffering, I saw, was closely bound up with the laws of family—in the strict sense of blood-relation-ship, and in the wider social sense of belonging to the human family. Just as *unearned good* came to one, so did *unearned ill*. A dentist's irresponsibility brought down con-sequences alike on the just and the unjust, and germs in an unhealthy clothes-room were not less dangerous in the case of a Christian.

Suppose, I said to myself, having no strength to say it to another, God did hold up the laws of cause and effect to spare His 'pet children', meaning in my visitors' sense, His Christian children, that would make religion a kind of insurance policy. Everyone would be Christian—for the wrong reason—*it would pay in bare terms of physical preservation.*

117

Laws of health, I saw, were impartial, and unalterable, and it was one's lifelong businesss to regard them.

I learned also in those days much about '*Invalid Bookery*', to borrow a nurse's term. I found it scarcely less important than invalid cookery. I read incessantly—three or four books on my bed at a time—biography, travel, poetry, theology, fiction. Like Pompey, I found I could 'lie in my bed in all four corners of the earth'.

And time passed, but unhappily my doctor had to say that in his opinion, and in the opinion of those with whom he had consulted, I would never work again.

I was in my middle twenties—eager for life and work—and I had no work, no health, and no money.

Yet it seemed to me as I faced things thoughtfully in the night watches that God might still have something for me to do. *I began to write.*

Said one:

> *He who has suffered much, knows many tongues.*
> *He can be understood, he understands*
> *The language of the countless ones who reach*
> *For sympathy with weak imploring hands. . . .*
> *There will be those who may require of you*
> *Help to go some first bewildering mile*
> *With grief and pain. God will have need of you*
> *As His interpreter that you may tell*
> *Them of the hope ahead, of the healing years,*
> *And of His love. Oh, learn the language well.*

I read over my first effort to Rene, at the end of many months. She was kind.

And the end was a book. I called it *Through Open Windows*. I did not know whether it was a very good book: I only knew that it had nothing to say about suffering, but that on every page it had something to say about faith and the kind of inner joy that I had found adequate.

Often now I am asked, 'What were the first essentials, in setting to write a book?' I would say a love of life, a love of people, a love of books, a love of words. And one needs, above all I am sure, a deeply-rooted love of sharing things—some lovely find, some little bit of truth, some human experience. And, of course, one needs to know the alphabet, and to be able to spell—to know, for instance, how many r's there are in 'terrible'. And it is rather useful to be on friendly terms with English grammar. There is, after all, a right and gracious way of saying things. A technical book needs exact technical terms, an adventure story short, sharp sentences, suggesting hasty movement, a descriptive book of the countryside needs more words of quiet colour, contentment and grace.

Good friends saw that first little book through the press. I shall remember always the strange emotion on first seeing a little bit of my soul tucked up between two covers of a book. So much, I knew, depended on the reader. 'The reader and the writer are one flesh; of their union the living book is made,' as Clemence Dane has said. 'Each book is a series of little pointed signs—essentially only that. It is for the reader to supply himself the forms and colours and sentiments to which these signs correspond. . . . Or if you prefer to put it otherwise, each word in the book is a magic finger that sets a fibre of our brain vibrating like a harp-string, and so evokes a note from the sounding-board of the soul.'

Some of those who discovered that little book in its early days, found in it something of eagerness and over-coming which matched their own hearts, and thirteen reprintings were called for, before the English publishing house took it over, that gives it life till this day.

It was made up simply enough—of letters slowly and patiently worked over when I was apart from 'the sweet, keen trouble of living'. And it proved such an extension of life that only in part were Mary Webb's words true for me: 'It is hard, if people are young and eager for action, to be chained by physical weakness. It is grievous to be forced to lead a life of contemplation when the heart is set upon roaming—to be placed upon a philosophical hillside when you are all afire to be down in the plain, amid the sweet, keen trouble of living.'

For its jacket and frontispiece I drew a silhouette of a girl seated at an open window. Never for one moment did I dream that one day a copy of that little sketch would hang in a church.

A minister, then unknown to me, wrote, after ten years. 'There are times when even the most optimistic of us get an attack of the "blues". I thought I would like to send you this remarkable account of a transformed life. Dorothy grew up with an elder brother and younger sister, and lacked nothing. Fond of reading, she had musical tastes, and was skilled at hand-work. She was tall, and more than passably good-looking. But up to reaching twenty-one she seemed aloof in the home, and even less easily approached by any outside the family.

'After a three-year absence from the district, I received a message telling me of her death. On arrival at the parents' home, there was a large company assembled; some had come long distances. The boy scouts formed a guard of honour. There were more people outside the church than the number of those able to gain admission. Absence from the district left me at a complete loss to account for the demonstration of affection at the passing of such a reserved young woman.

'Later, in the home, in conversation with Dorothy's mother, I made an effort to unravel the mystery. Her mother, without a word, took a home-made picture from the wall. It showed a young woman sitting at an open window. It was a copy of the frontispiece of *Through Open*

Windows, and a piece of verse from the book was underneath:

> *Stretch out your hand and take the world's wide gift*
> *Of Joy and Beauty. . . .*
> *Open the windows of your wondering heart*
> *To God's supreme creation.*

'In the interval of years the miracle had happened. A
new spirit had come to Dorothy; the icy cold and reserve
had been banished: life had begun anew. Work in the
Church, and teaching in the Sunday-school had been
joyously undertaken; and the service of organist in the
Sunday-school. The boy scouts had found a god-mother in
Dorothy, as with full heart and soul she entered into all
the worth-while activities of the community.

'*If your book,*' added the minister, '*has done no more than
this, how worthwhile it has been!*'

Dorothy's copy of my frontispiece now hangs beside her
plaque of remembrance in the Church that she loved and
served. When I had a speaking appointment in the township, I was taken to see it.

So again, the thing 'that seemed not good, was turned
to good'.

At the end of my two years of illness, I summoned up
courage to ring the doctor's bell, and ask for my bill. I
shall never forget that evening, nor his words: he said
quite simply: 'There is no bill. Between those of us who
have examined you, we have only had one other case like
yours—and that other is not here now. By rights, you
ought not to be here, either. But for your faith, let me
say, and your spirit, you wouldn't be here. *And no doctor
will take a fee for that.*'

Thus did I learn in a dark, bitter place to walk this
common way, with a deeper sense of responsibility toward
the good, sweet things of life!

XIII

In time I was persuaded back to the Mission. My journey from now on, I knew, had to be made in company with a scarred heart. It was not easy to attempt a part-time job when I had done a full one. I had constantly to husband my strength, and to be mindful of steps and hills.

The benefits of a sea-trip had many times been mentioned, but the dream of seeing England still seemed remote, until one day I went to Cook's and came home with a handful of leaflets.

Rene's eyes shone with eagerness until I outlined plans. Then her first reaction was: 'Don't rush me! Don't rush me!' But I did rush her: I rushed myself, I rushed Cook's. Added to what benefit the trip might bring me, I wanted to be in England for the breaking of the spring.

We sat down like eager children, and counted out our money. We were sorry it wasn't more, we were glad it wasn't less. But I discovered that I could sell some of my library, that I could cut hair at sixpence a time, that I could walk tram-sections, and work the summer holidays through. A tiny insurance that I had begun as a child, came due, and when my father heard of my plans, he sent me a gift.

'*Merely to be alive,*' we told ourselves, using the words of Walter de la Mare, '*is adventure enough in a world like this, so erratic and disjoined, so lovely and so odd and mysterious and profound.*'

We got ourselves each a tiny note-book, and ruled up black columns for spending, and red columns for credit. Then we divided the months at our disposal into the money at our disposal. We meant to tot up at the end of each week; we knew we couldn't go quite bankrupt in a week. We even hoped that by travelling modestly, tramping through the English countryside, doing an occasional camp job or lecture, to have something to put into those red columns for extras—a trip into Holland when the tulips were aflame, a week or two in France, a glimpse of Switzerland.

And so it turned out—but far, far better than our dreams!

There are, of course, several schools of packing. There are those who like to begin a week or so before-hand; there are the people who throw in things at the last minute, and hopefully call on their neighbours to come and sit on the lid; there are the careful packers, insatiable consumers of tissue-paper. And there are those who take quantities of things they ought not to have taken, and leave behind things that they ought to have taken.

I am by nature one of those who likes to get things well in hand. But this time, I scarcely had a choice; I was running a Children's Health Camp till within a day or two of departure, and most of the task fell on Rene.

Ronald Selby Wright has said 'the people with whom we travel are much *more* important than the place to which we travel'. I was doubly fortunate.

As the warm sunlight of a summer's day lessened, our good-byes were said, and our ship pulled out. Soon the upturned faces of friends became indistinguishable as the distance between wharf and ship widened.

Our last glimpse of New Zealand was an outline of soft blues, and a very lovely remembrance of one's land it was, to carry in the heart for a year.

Our first sight of Australia was of the buttress brown of Sydney Heads, as we came up on deck two-and-a-half days later. And there was no missing the great bridge. Would the *Awatea's* masts really clear it? Our upturned eyes bespoke the question. Next moment we were underneath, a diamond-shaped mark indicating the centre of the great structure. One standing beside us said the mark measured seven feet—it looked inches.

We need not have worried: the high-water clearance of the greatest single-arched bridge in the world, stood at a hundred-and-seventy feet. Its size was so deceptive that it was hard to believe it was two-and-three-quarter miles long, including approaches.

'How wonderful,' I exclaimed, 'it must have been to see the two giant spans come together. 'Yes,' replied Rene, 'it's always hard enough to get two sides of a collar to fit!'

Sydney Harbour we found incredibly lovely as we sailed into it, looked down upon it by night, or crossed it by ferry. Anthony Trollope's words rose often to mind. 'I have seen nothing equal to it,' said he, 'nothing second to it. It is so inexpressibly lovely that it makes a man ask himself whether it would not be worth his while to move his household goods to the East Coast of Australia, in order that he might look at it as long as he can look at anything.'

Trollope's enthusiasm, of course, had been variously expressed. The harbour stretched a hundred-and-eighty odd miles, in bays and deep waterways.

The city itself, centred in the noisy canyons of Martin Place, George, Castlereagh, King and Wynyard Streets, spreading out into densely populated be-gardened suburbs, along the water-front, in and out of a thousand bays, seemed almost to have happened before anyone had time to think how it ought to happen. It might have been the most beautifully laid-out city in the world! Nature provided so much! Stretching out over a hundred-thousand acres, the city and suburbs, we found, were home to a million-and-a-quarter people.

My mind flew back to that other January day, when Capt. Phillip, moored in Botany Bay, was greeted by the natives 'making a noise and lifting up their spears'.

In some ways, Phillip was plainly ahead of his time. Despite the number of convicts, he saw his task as the founding of a nation, not as the keeping of a prison. Even the great Pitt failed to see the possibilities that Phillip's far-seeing mind envisaged. 'In point of expense,' said the great statesman, 'no cheaper mode of disposing of convicts could be found.'

Traces of those inhumane days remain—at places like Hartley Court House up in the hills, or in old records and newspapers.

Even in the sight of God there were cruel differences, so that when St. Phillip's Church got its Communion Plate, two sets were provided, 'gold, for the free, and copper for the bond'. One newspaper of 1798 wrote—ten years after Governor Phillip landed—'The theatre at Botany Bay is entirely built by convicts, and cost about one hundred pounds. With singular propriety, the gallery is the largest part of the house. The admission is one shilling, which is paid either in money, or in flour or meat!" Another paper recorded the trial of one who 'had endeavoured to introduce his hand into another's pocket for an unlawful purpose'. Among 'shipping intelligence' and 'advertisements of merchandise', were occasional notes of a more desperate and personal character. 'Whereas,' one read, 'my wife Mary Ann Wardle (formerly known as Mary Ann Dunlevy), a blooming damsel on the verge of fifty, of tall stature and without front teeth, has absconded from her home; this is to caution all persons from paying any monies to the said Mary Ann Wardle on my account . . .'
Poor Mary Ann Wardle!

The years had wrought incredible changes. As we rattled in from the suburbs on electric trains, and jostled our way along the crowded streets, it was hard to believe that there had ever been a time when four-and-a-half acres in George Street—now in the throbbing heart of the city—had changed hands for a 'chest of tea, two bags of sugar, a couple of pieces of broadcloth, twelve gallons of port wine, six gallons of Hollands, a saddle and bridle, a set of harness, a single-barrelled fowling-piece, four bags of shot, and twenty-five pounds of tobacco.' Within the life-time of the 'seller's widow', the same acres had changed hands for fifty-thousand sovereigns!

Sydney grown so large, set on the edge of an almost empty continent, no longer represented to the newcomer, the true spirit of Australia.

As newcomers, our only breach of the law was not serious, though lives hung on issues scarcely as important in old convict days: we had too many chocolates. Friends had treated us too well. 'A haversack filled with chocolates. Far too many for two people,' said the customs officials with genial immovability. 'You can't land them here without paying duty. We'll transfer them for you, if you like.' So our 'contraband' was among our luggage, when our English ship left Woolloomooloo.

Woolloomooloo! Does any traveller ever manage to spell it without a little friendly prompting? If our stay could have been stretched out twice its length, I think I might have managed it: I was just winning through from amusement to confidence when it was time to go. Dr. Thomas Wood, English musician and composer, set down Woolloomooloo as a good sea-shanty wasted:

Woolloomooloo ba-lah, be-lay,
Woolloomooloo belay!

Our next call was at Hobart, in Tasmania, to load

126

apples. This allowed us two days ashore—two beautiful February days. Life ran placidly in Hobart. We seemed to have entered another world. Friends met us and took us away up Mount Wellington, for the view, and up to Silver Falls for a picnic.

Hobart had shared in the unhappy past of convict days, but to us it was nowhere apparent, save in the relics treasured in the two fine old churches we visited, and in the historic room of the museum. There we saw the crude 'ducking-box', used on the yard-arm of a convict ship, for 'obstreperous passengers', and the cat-o'-nine-tails, and instruments of 'man's inhumanity to man'. We read that prisoners 'were not permitted to speak or sing or make any noise other than that necessary to their work'. But surely they needed no threatening notice to keep them from singing—what was there to sing about? For evidence there were the leg-irons with which they were grimly chained together. A copy of a printed notice ordered them to stand for Grace before and after meals, on pain of punishment. Thankful for such meals? And under such conditions? Even when they were marched to church, they went each wearing a linen cowl—a bag-like contrivance with two holes in it—and they dare not speak even to the next man, lest he should be a warder. One couldn't help wondering what a minister of the Gospel found to say under such circumstances.

But all such painful things plainly belonged to the past.

The gracious city of Melbourne we loved at sight. Van Dyke's words were constantly on our lips. 'He who plants a tree is a servant of God.' Melbourne, we felt sure, was full of the servants of God. No one could walk her streets, linger in her parks, or traverse her leafy avenues and not feel it so.

For all that she was smaller than Melbourne, Adelaide

127

we found to have a grace unforgettable. Her North Terrace, girdled with trees, and adorned with her university, art gallery and library, composed one of the world's lovely boulevards. But in February the temperature of Adelaide was hotter than anything we had ever experienced.

And Perth was hotter still. I wanted to make a little sound like a cicada.

The first settlers could have known nothing of our trials. Their arrival was in winter, and one of their number had left a grim record: 'The all-pervading sandiness of the long stretch of low-lying coast, reduced the ardour of the bravest of the pioneer band. Few or no tents,' she recorded, 'had been provided for their accommodation. . . . The weather, even for winter, being unusually severe, the unfortunate women and children were exposed to the most harassing privations, and had frequently to sleep under umbrellas as the only covering. Champagne cases, pianos and even carriages were later used in improvizing temporary dwellings. Only with the greatest difficulty could these unfortunate people, unused as they were to rough colonial life, light fires for cooking purposes.'

Leaving Australia, things aboard banged in the night, cabin doors slammed, and luggage slithered about the floor. Despite the size and comfort of our ship compared with those tiny vessels that came in the early days, we found ourselves asking several unanswerable questions. Was the sea, we asked, more treacherous than it used to be? Or did those early-comers have a different kind of courage, and endurance?

XIV

LIFE at sea seemed an existence apart—the past all behind, the future all to come. Even in the old days when the voyage between England and the new world took four *months* instead of four weeks, shipping companies pointed out in printed leaflets how the time might be spent. 'Some people,' they began brightly, 'consider that the time must of necessity pass very heavily, which is altogether a mistake; for it is really inconceivable with what rapidity weeks, nay months, seem to disappear during a voyage, especially *if a person be moderately partial to literary pursuits!*' Delightful phrase! I counted myself fortunate to be more than 'moderately partial to literary pursuits'. 'The very regularity, or as it is termed monotony, of the life one leads, tends to make the days appear short,' the old shipping notice added, 'and when it is considered how many sources of recreation are supplied by reading, chess, etc., it is seldom that anyone, save the mere idler, will find the day too long. If there should be any person, who, instead of employing his time rationally, thinks of nothing but eating and drinking, no uncommon circumstance, he may expect to feel enough of the *tedium vitae* to make him wish himself on shore again.'

My 'literary pursuits' were helped by an excellent library.

Day after day the screw turned, the deck games gained in excitement, the meal-times came and went, the sweethearts strolled, and leaned over the bow in the moonlight. Sunday reduced the tempo a little, and many who had not been in church for years, put on their best, and selfconsciously crowded into the saloon to hear the Captain read the lessons and prayers.

One blue afternoon news came round that we were to call at the Cocos Islands. It was very exciting. We began to dig in our memories for what little we knew of the islands. We told each other authoritatively and enthusiastically that the Cocos Islands were the scene of H.M.A.S. *Sydney's* exploit in World War I, when she chased to her death the German cruiser *Emden*.

To this insufficient information, the Captain added that the islands—a mere cluster of coral atolls—housed, in addition to the small native population, a cable-station and twenty-six white men. The loneliness was too great for white women and children.

Only very rarely were the men visited by a home-going ship, with the chance of an out-going mail. And we sent them a message to tell them of our plan to call.

Next afternoon, we spotted the islands—a little world of fringy green set gloriously, with a tremendous surf breaking on the coral reefs. The native huts were visible only where silhouetted against the sky.

As our great ship slowed down, some distance out, we all crowded to the rail. Three boats were seen approaching. As chief treasure they carried a small barrel, sealed and be-flagged, containing their letters. Our men produced a second barrel, filled with chocolates, smokes and magazines, and bearing a flag of a different colour.

Both barrels were soon bobbing on the waves. The exchange effected, we made ready to leave; but before we parted, a great fellow from the islands stood in his tiny boat—looking for all the world like Robinson Crusoe, with a ginger beard, and a red handkerchief about his neck, and with his two arms upraised, called out clearly the only message we heard during our visit—'Give our love to King George!'

The romance of the visit was coloured, for many of us no doubt, by those stories of youth that we had read in the long grass, *Robinson Crusoe*, *Kidnapped* and *Treasure Island*. The ghosts of Long John Silver and his crew, it was not hard to believe, still roved the seas. We might, it seemed, at any minute, raise hands to eyes to catch sight of a black vessel flying the Jolly Roger, the Black Flag, or more sinister, no flag at all.

Our next excitement was crossing the Equator. And then the new, *and more or less familiar world was behind us—the old world ahead.*

We loved Colombo, and it did not take us long to know that we were in a world incredibly ancient—a world of slashed sun-scorched roadways, and covered markets, gay with a thousand colours. Now, when travellers talk of the East, I can recall that fascinating glimpse. I have not climbed Greenland's icy mountains, nor visited India's coral strand; but I have lifted up my nose to 'the spicy breezes that blow soft o'er Ceylon's isle'.

We came next to Aden, that parched, rock-tortured town on the edge of the ancient desert, where lies, it is claimed, the body of Cain, the slayer of Abel.

In the crowded market-street, with awnings as colourful as the tent of Abraham, and as ancient in design, were Arab, Persian, Indian and Somali tradesmen.

On our way up to the hot crater town, we met a little knot of Mohammedan women, heavily veiled, save for a tiny piece of gauze over the eyes. Coming back, our vehicle collided with a camel and his stubborn master, and only got away after much cursing—an Arab cursing can sound pretty fearsome!

By evening, our ship replenished with oil that had come by pipe-line, was ready to leave. The hot fury of the day past, we sat on deck, about us the soft heliotropes and mauves of the desert.

Rene wakened me from the sweet depths of sleep, as we made our midnight entry into the Red Sea. I was not sure what I was meant to see; what I did see was a particularly black kind of pitch blackness.

On Good Friday when dawn was breaking we passed into the Gulf of Suez. Across the desert was a soft, mauvy colour. To the west were soft purple mountains, near at hand a few Bible-story boats and flat Eastern houses.

Terrifically fierce heat embraced us as we made our way through the Canal. All along the way there was much to see, the little palm-fringed settlements on the canal-side a special joy.

Belloc's words were continually on my lips as I peered out from beneath the grateful awnings of the ship:

O Africa, mysterious land,
Surrounded by a lot of sand. . . !

It was a dark velvety night when we reached Port Said, and near midnight before we got ashore.

The ancient port will always be associated in my mind with the sight and sound of an endless chain of coal-heavers, silhouetted against the moon. As they made their steep ascent of a nearby gangway, they chanted a dirge not easy to be cast out of the mind. On and on through the night went their endless chain of labour, on and on through the night, their dirge of labour.

Just on twelve we had dealings with a native boy with beads to sell. We were in no mood to buy; as quickly as he put his wares over our necks, we cast them off. 'Too late!' I said, thinking of the hour, 'It's far too late!'

Half-a-mile distant in the lighted shopping area, to our surprise, half-an-hour later we turned a corner with the throng, and came upon the same boy. With the amazing memory developed by such boy touts from the shops, his face lit up in an instant as he approached us smilingly with, '*O Mrs. Too-Late!*'

By the time we sighted ancient Crete we were seeking out woollen jackets. It was gloriously crisp and clear up on deck; looking down on the soft, blue hills, the distant mountains snow-capped, the blue, blue Mediterranean lapping us round. The mere mention of Fair Havens to the South sent us speeding back to St. Paul's record of his winter there.

At sunset Mount Etna came into view. And as we approached the coast of Sicily, she cast off her filmy mantle. The nearness of land was exciting, as we zig-zagged through the narrow Straits of Messina. On the morrow—entrancing thought—we should walk in Italy.

But before we forsook the deck that night, an unforgettable sight was vouchsafed. The ship's lights extinguished, our eyes gradually became accustomed to the soft darkness, and we picked out Stromboli, quite near, rising cone-like from the sea. Presently, she began to cast molten lava into the darkness. And great burning chunks rolled sizzling down the cone's side. With the vivid reflection, and heavy roll of smoke from the crater, it was an awe-inspiring sight. Many a traveller passes without seeing such a display.

It was an uncanny thought that people were, at that moment, sleeping unalarmed on the non-eruptive side. On several occasions, we learned, boats had had to be hurriedly summoned to take them off—fisher-folk, and peasants from the mainland mostly, who cultivate vines on the small patches of fertile soil.

By breakfast time we were sailing into the Bay of Naples, Vesuvius smoking ominously in the background—our third volcano. The ancient saying: *Vidi Napoli e poi muori:* 'See Naples and die,' suddenly had significance.

The flowing capes of the *Fascisti* were the most colourful sight as we came ashore. It was hard to believe that we were not back-stage at an Italian Opera.

We tramped the streets. The quaint open horse carriages passed us. We drove to the famous Cathedral of San Gennaro; we photographed historic buildings; we made our way out to Pompeii. At the roadside were spring wild-flowers, poppies and marigolds, and over pergolas, beautiful trailing mauve wistaria. Almonds and cherries and vines were a joy, and the people seemed gay.

Pompeii held surprise. I never thought I could enjoy 'dead things' so much, but everything was fraught with such human interest. We traced the chariot-wheel marks in the streets; we crossed on stepping-stones that had served pedestrians before the ancient city was overwhelmed. We paused to wonder at the city's central-heating system, and to muse over the Theatre of Tragedy, and the Theatre of Comedy.

And night brought us back to Naples—to its ancient squalor and beauty and song. 'I hold,' says Maurice Baring, 'that in many ways, Naples is the most characteristic, the most Italian, of all Italy's cities. It is the most exaggeratedly Italian of them all. It is there you see the best of blue skies, the yellowest of yellow houses, where you hear Italian talk at its most garrulous, Italian smells at their most pungent, and Italian song at its most nasal sentimental pitch, those squalling, pathetic, imploring, slightly flat love songs. At Florence, you think; at Rome, you pray; at Venice, you love; at Naples, you look!'

In a very short time we were savouring the delights of early spring in southern France. Never will I forget our motor run out beyond Nice, up into the hills above Villefrance, to La Turbie. Never will I forget the winding way, and the little villages, and the delicious almond cakes. As my fellow-New Zealander, Katherine Mansfield carried it in her heart to the end, I shall always remember La Turbie. 'I can't spell it,' said she in one of her letters, 'and am ashamed to ask, but it's up, up high on the tops of the mountains. It's a tiny, ancient Roman town, incredibly ancient! With old bits with pillars and capitals—Oh, dear—it is so lovely. The road winds and winds to get there round and round the mountains.'

That evening, for us the sun went down toward the frontier of Italy, the coastline away in the mauvy-blue distance, with its castles and forts. It held an unimaginable beauty. Then the tiny lights came out.

We spent an hour or two in the streets and tree-filled gardens of Monte Carlo. And late—picking our way through the quaintly ill-lighted streets and alleys of the port with steps and steep places leading down—we made our way back to the ship.

Next day brought us to Toulon, and its market-street—on either side tall cream houses, with green shutters, many of them with strings of washing hanging out.

Lovely bunches of lilac, and fresh produce from the countryside lay stacked on the improvised stalls, cheek-by-jowl with olives, shrimps, radishes, handkerchiefs and almond cakes. For a few centimes, I carried away a beautiful bunch of lilac. Added to its dewy fragrance was a sentimental value: our old home in the village was called 'The Lilacs'. Eight or nine great trees grew there, all the years that I knew it.

Gibraltar was something of an anti-climax. True, it was Sunday, and some parts of the fortress town were shut. We had a ride over the cobbles in a *gharry*, but for the rest, Maurice Baring's four lines sum up my memories as well as anything I might write:

Gibraltar.
Most people have been there.
For those who haven't, it looks
Exactly as it does in books.

A few more days—busy days with suit-cases and packing—
and we were peering through the fog for the white cliffs of
Dover, the fog horn made its complaint 'like a god in
pain'.

XV

I⊤ took us a little while to shake off the depression that
settled on our spirits between Tilbury Docks and London.
'The sublimest thing I know,' said Edward Thomas, 'is
the sea, and after that London.' As the stewards trundled
our bags up to the top of the gangway that April morning,
we were in a mood to agree with him. But before we could
leave the sea, and get to London, we had to traverse the
dreary man-made waste in between. Never before had we
seen so many back yards looking so exactly alike—with
little lines of dismal washing; never before had we seen
so many streets of front doors looking so exactly alike—
with numbers, steps and knockers, repeating themselves
endlessly like incurable hiccoughs.

The taxis at St. Pancras station were our next surprise.
So this was London! These tiny back yards, these
ancient box-like, toy-like vehicles, driven by cloth-capped
knowledgeable gnomes. So this was London—this was the
London of Pepys; the London of the beloved Lamb; this
was Dickens's London, introduced a dozen times; this was
the London of Johnson, that gusty old genius. His words
came instantly to mind: 'When a man is tired of London he
is tired of life; for there is in London all that life can afford.'

But anyone who reads English history, before she had
any literature, enters the most real London. Interest in
her was already deep when Roman soldiers, with a handful of nails, put up a Cross on Calvary. And the most
easily-recognized thing in her midst, we found, was
reminder of that tragedy, that triumph—the cross-tipped
dome of St. Paul's.

Here, we told ourselves wonderingly—in this same city

—Roman emperors had marched their legions; here, enemies had snatched a little building-space from the wilds; here minstrels had sung their songs; scholars and saints had walked; and good men and women had been put to death. It was all here—the long tale of the centuries, in glory and greatness!

To us in that April morning, much of it seemed familiar —the great dome of St. Paul's, Big Ben, the graceful towers of Westminster, the Bridges across the Thames, St. Martin-in-the-Fields, and the 'never-ceasing torrents of the Strand'. We were at long last surrounded by things we felt we understood. We had come 'Home'.

But London, we soon realized, was a centre of the world's business, too. Beside my plate, on the lunch-table, lay a slim telegram. And in response to its call, we took a bus, and set off for City Road.

There, as we stepped out of the office of my publishers, by the merest chance—one in London's eight millions— was a friend whom I had seen off from New Zealand months before. He was staying miles out in the country, but business had brought him into London.

We talked. Then shaking off the concerns of business, he asked: 'What are you doing next? There's a good opera on at Sadler's Wells.' (How strange that name sounded: how familiar it was to sound in the twelve months following. Indeed, for the rest of our lives.)

He dived, a little ahead of us, down into the Underground. It was important, it seemed, that we should hurry. He did not suspect that we'd never been on an escalator; we did not stop to explain that we had never been on an Underground. It might not have helped just then to have told us that each year five-hundred-and-fifty-three millions of London's human moles make their journeys this way; it might not have helped to have told us that there were a hundred-and-sixty-five escalators on

138

the system—since we had never been on one. But what would have helped—and it could hardly have taken more than a minute with the pocket Underground map—would have been an outline of how the system worked, and what all those bewildering passages and lights and rushing noises were for.

But there was no time. Everybody at that hour was rushing—and we had to rush too.

We descended the escalator at the Bank, and awaited the train. It came in, with a noise that could only suggest an on-coming earthquake, or a volcanic eruption. As far as we could see, there was no name to indicate destination, and no guard to ask 'Where do you want to go to?' or shout 'Are you coming?' Automatic doors opened—as if in Alice's Wonderland—and a stream of humanity burst out. We took our places. The sliding doors snapped to, and we were off. In a moment, we were rattling past funny names that appeared and disappeared before we could grasp them: 'Moorgate', and 'Old Street', and 'Angel'. What funny names! Why the Angel? But there was no time.

Once above the ground again, we discovered that dusk was about us. 'Come on!' said our friend, 'Sadler's Wells is no great distance.' He was not quite sure of his direction. We looked at the names on one or two streets. But we arrived only to find that they'd changed the programme. Distrusting the first bill-board, our friend consulted the others. 'Look, they've changed it,' he said. 'What shall we do?'

What we did—after two minutes' consultation—was to undo all that we'd done—and more.

The Undergrounds were not quite so terrifying this time, though just as bewildering. We came up at Aldwych. How we got there, I had not the least idea, but presently one fact presented itself to my mind of which I was perfectly sure: outside the Aldwych Theatre Jane Eyre was billed. We took our places in the queue.

Now that we had stopped rushing, we had some time to fill in. An old man in a rusty coat, with a rook on his back, came to entertain us—and collect our pennies—and so did a couple of urchins who turned marvellous cart-wheels, and an old hag with a wheezy voice and a gramo-phone on her knee. After a time, two policemen put in an appearance, and the urchins vanished.

Another surprise, in this London full of surprises, awaited us when we entered. Hardly had we taken our seats, when we looked up to see in beautiful old English lettering—where on a scroll in Church, we might read 'Worship the Lord in the Beauty of Holiness'—a scroll: 'Beware of Pickpockets!'

This was London!

Ten minutes before the play ended, our friend suddenly remembered he had to catch a last train to the country in eighteen minutes. 'Do you girls think you can find your way?' he whispered in a voice that completely obliterated the climax of the play. 'You are no great distance from the Club. I could draw you a map on the back of an envelope.'

We bade him good-bye outside the theatre, stood a moment to match a street-name up on a tall building with a pencilled name on our envelope. We were all right!

A few minutes after twelve we turned the key in our room at the Club—on the sixth floor. We were safe! Sitting there, was our be-labelled luggage—comfortably reassuring. *So this was London!*

> *Not by appointment do we meet delight and joy,*
> *They heed not our expectancy;*
> *But at the corner of the street of life,*
> *They, on a sudden, clasp us with a smile.*

For the next few days we made no further attempt to come to terms with the Underground: we went everywhere on foot, studying road-signs, and grasping our guide-book.

The first morning we came suddenly on one of the loveliest glimpses London has to offer in the spring—the daffodils under the trees in Lincoln's Inn Fields. The branches of the trees and tiny twigs were as black as ebony, but at their tips, the tiniest green was breaking. We caught sight of them first, between tall buildings, and with the daffodils beneath, they were a sight to catch the breath. Despite our astonishment, there was something so right about this vision of loveliness.

This was London!

Later that same day, we found ourselves part of a delighted crowd outside old St. Clement Danes in the Strand. The annual service of the Oranges and Lemons was being held. Each happy child guest from the East End, leaving the old Church, decorated for the day with great boughs of oranges and lemons, was being presented with an orange in one hand, and in the other a lemon. We were close enough to study expressions, and we saw, with some amusement, that the little ones knew well enough what they were going to do with their oranges —they grasped them eagerly—but were in some doubt about what to do with the lemons!

And all the while, in merry mood, the old bells rang out the song of childhood: 'Oranges and Lemons, the Bells of St. Clements!'

So this was London, too! Yes, in very truth, this *was* London!

A night or two later, by a happy chance, we found ourselves part of another piece of London's past.

The night was fine, and at a few minutes to nine

we were finding our way again to Lincoln's Inn Fields.

We had known a little about the Curfew as long as we could remember anything—that when naked lights had been used in the homes and workshops of the people, it had been a good thing to put them all out at nine o'clock, and go to bed. The Curfew had been instituted to tell them when it was nine o'clock. After that, it had been judged an offence to be in the streets. This much we knew, as a piece of school-book history. But that the Curfew was still rung from Lincoln's Inn Fields, was only one more of London's surprises.

Chatting with the old doorkeeper on that first day when we lighted on the daffodils, I asked him about the Curfew. Yes, it was still rung, he assured me, at nine o'clock each night. And the great oaken door was closed at sundown.

'Does anyone ever come to see you ring the Curfew?' I asked.

'No, no one.'

'*Could* anyone come?' I persisted.

Guessing my thoughts, the old doorkeeper left me in no doubt about the matter.

'Of course, the door will be shut. But I think I could show you a little hole in the wall where you could come through. There will be a bobby on the road outside, but you could give him a nod—I'll tell him you're coming.'

So there we were: Wednesday, eight minutes to nine! We had come through the little hole in the wall. The old doorkeeper was awaiting us in his tiny office.

There was time, yet. Consulting his watch, and replacing it carefully in his pocket, he led us across the court-yard, by the light of a torch, and up a staircase, to where a rope was hanging from the ceiling above us. It was totally dark, save for the tiny yellow glow of the torch.

Suddenly, standing there, he asked: 'Would you like to ring it?'

'Oh,' we replied, with some diffidence, 'we had hardly thought of that.'

'It's fifty strokes,' said he, 'fifty strokes—one stroke— and count two under your breath for a pause—then forty-eight strokes—count two under your breath for a pause—then your fiftieth stroke.'

'Fifty strokes,' I said. 'I think you'd better put your hand on the rope for a start.' And he did.

And that April night, with unreasonable joy, we rang the Curfew over London!

Coming down, I said: 'I suppose nobody takes any notice of it nowadays.'

'No, ma'am,' he answered me, 'no—unless it doesn't go.'

'Are there times, then,' I queried, 'when it doesn't go?'

'Oh, no—no, ma'am,' said he, 'only about six years ago, one night I forgot the time. And a score of folk or more came up to see what was the matter.'

Something would be the matter with London, if she dozed—or in any way forgot her past. It is her past, mingled inextricably with her present, that endears her to us so much.

Modern triumphs of business, science, and the arts she has, too; but she is old now, and doesn't need to boast about these things like a youngster city of a few hundred years.

XVI

GREAT and constant tides of traffic flow into London—
closely on the ebb of the night's life comes in the new day's
activity.

S. P. B. Mais entitled one of his books: *It isn't far
from London.* Now that we had grown familiar with the
Underground that had so terrified us at first, we remembered his quoted dialogue with the ticket-window man:

> *It's 'Monument' and 'Charing Cross',*
> *And 'Kensington' and 'Kew';*
> *It's 'Colindale' and 'Maida Vale',*
> *And 'Sloane' and 'Waterloo';*
> *A touch of a key, and a ticket shoots out,*
> *And our change clangs down a metal spout,*
> *And we grab it and run*
> *For the nine-twenty-one.*
> *(There isn't much time for the graces) . . .*
> *Faces and faces and faces,*
> *And all of them blank as a wall—*
> *O clerk at the ticket window, aren't*
> *You sick of us all?*
>
> *And you might have tended sheep on a hill*
> *And known each one as a friend;*
> *Or gone afloat in a white-winged boat,*
> *And counted the stars without end,*
> *Which are very much nicer things to see*
> *Than the faces of Brown and Jones and me,*
> *As we bustle along*
> *Through the waiting throng,*
> *For we're all in a deuce of a hurry.*

Hurry and scurry and flurry.
And life is a jostling queue—
O clerk of the ticket window, is
This the best you can do?

The ticket-clerk, of course, might have had a wife and six children in one of the suburbs that his trains passed through. He might have loved London so much that he could hardly tear his heart away, even for a few days at the beach in August.

But we could leave London in April; we could seek the country in spring, when it was breaking green, and a thousand miracles were in the woods.

We could take 'bus, to rid ourselves of the City and its long arms of suburbs. We could sleep the first night under our friend's roof in Kent, and next morning start off, haversacks on back, in search of England.

'England,' we remembered Baldwin's words, 'is the country, and the country is England. England comes to me,' he had said, 'through my various senses—through certain imperishable scents . . . And the sounds of England are the tinkle of the hammer on the anvil in the country smithy, the corn-crake on a dewy morning, the sound of the scythe against the whetstone, and the sight of a plough team coming over the brow of a hill. . . .' *But we wanted to complete his enchanting list for ourselves. . . .*

In no time, we were on our way. Our haversacks seemed heavy, but 'the burden one likes is cheerfully borne'. We meant to make our first day a pilgrimage to Canterbury town. We meant to stay at Youth Hostels, where we would be welcome for a modest shilling a night.

A lark rose overhead. The hedges were sweet. We fell under the spell of our map. There were little red triangles that meant Hostels at the long days' close. There were little wiggles that meant rivers and streams; there were marks that meant woods, and others that meant churches and inns. We turned over with pleasure, as we walked, Yeats's words: 'Did you ever think that the roads are the only things that are endless?'

A blackbird sang at the end of our first five miles—a song all the sweeter for being like a phrase from a song countrymen used to sing. Distance and speed were nothing to us. We would traverse five miles or fifteen, sixteen or twenty-six, as our hearts dictated. We were out to discover England, and had chosen, we believed, the only real way in which it could be done.

We went down through blossoming Kent, on into the sweet heart of Sussex. We found wild flowers in the woods, and dewdrops in the bosom of a leaf. We tramped the Downs, saturated with sun and air, and when the long twilight closed in, we found a hostel or an inn.

On up into Wiltshire we went, consulting our map: down into Devon and Somerset, where men and women carry into their speech the broad beautiful undulations of their countryside; down into Cornwall, where there are little bays and sweet salty places that refuse the consolation of grass, herb and tree. Round into Dorset we came— Dorset so ancient, that every breeze could tell a secret forgotten to living men; on up into Hampshire, green and beautiful—and so again to London.

All the way we found lovers of the same simple way of journeying, like my friend Ann. 'Did you come from So-and-so to-day?' they asked. 'And are you going on to-morrow? Go by the higher of the two paths where you come to the parting in the way, and you'll come to a toll gate. We came that way to-day. At the top of the valley, behind a white gate is a farmhouse where they serve wonderful cream teas. We thought you mightn't know.' So they helped us on our way.

As we looked at our maps, south of England place-names walked up and down in our hearts with the fascination of poetry. So many peoples had crossed her soil, leaving scraps of names in unexpected places like markers in a paper-chase—the Celts, the Romans, the Saxons, Danes, Norwegians, Normans, the Flemings, the Huguenots.

The very atmosphere breathed content—and next moment, without any contradiction, a strange curiosity about those who had passed that way before us. We lived with our maps, and loved them, till they became pleasantly dog-eared, and folded in all sorts of odd places they were never meant to be folded in; yet we knew that Edward Thomas was right: 'This is not the South Country which measures about two hundred miles from east to west and fifty from north to south. In some ways it is incomparably larger than any country that was ever mapped, since upon nothing less than the infinite can the spirit disport itself.'

So we came to old inns with names like the titles of books in a well-mellowed library. We talked with fishermen in little rocky coves, and farmers in great spready barns. We worshipped in great cathedrals—Canterbury, Wells, Salisbury, Exeter, Chichester, Winchester—and found inspiration and quiet of spirit in little country churches. Many a foundation upon which these earthly poems in stone were raised could witness to a thousand years of use. The fabric decays, but it is rebuilt, enlarged sometimes, sometimes changed in form, but never for a day ceasing to exist. To come to them, to worship within them, to walk about them, was to know a beauty on the edge of pain.

The beauty of their faith
Here flowers in stone,
Those ancient craftsmen

147

Of this western shire,
Built for God's glory
Rather than their own.

We of this latter day
Can but admire
Their work. We cannot hope
To equal them, until
We imitate their faith,
Deserve their skill.

Every morning as we journeyed, the sun making our shadows long in the roadway, the birds sang matins. No rain fell, but the country was sweet. We rested on road-sides, as the sun climbed high, and took our meals with the simplicity of pilgrims or tramps. We talked with old men in tiny villages where the great army of invaders—the tourists terrible with cameras—never come. We hung over bridges—bridges that 'even more than roads, are the symbols of man's conquest of nature. A bridge,' says Buchan, 'is concerned with the most beautiful of natural things, running water . . . .'

There was some truth in what he said. There might be a dozen roads, but they all came to a point at the river crossing. History, social, economic and military, clus-tered thickly about the bridges of those southern towns and citadels. Southern England's legacy of bridges is rich. Her streams—hurrying down from moors and valleys; her woody rivers on their way to the sea, have all been bridged to meet her needs. She has little humped-back bridges, and pack-horse bridges, and romantic and historic struc-tures of lofty grace.

We came occasionally, of course, to notice-boards offering 'This Magnificent Site', 'This Desirable Site', and faced the unpleasant fact that another part of the ancient and lovely south was turning to an ugly sophistication.

Despite the holiday resorts of the hard-pressed—the hordes that feel they must go down to the sea again—and the homes of the mercenary-minded, living in the country, out of touch with the country—there were rich and lovely things to remember. The blue smoke rising from chimneys at dusk; the blackbird on topmost bough; the ploughman coming up the furrowed slope; the tall spires uplifted, like the aspirations of man, against the tapestry of branches and bursting buds.

'*I find I am fully and most abundantly alive when walking in the countryside, either in solitude or in selected company.*'

As a rule I have little love for the ubiquitous writer who can cover a dozen counties and a dozen centuries in a week, and write a book about it. But at the end of weeks, and miles, with my haversack and my good companion, I had to write a book myself, for the easing of my spirit. It was full of old shoes, and meals by the way, and sound sleep under cottage eaves. I called it: *When We Two Walked*.

XVII

In London we were fortunate in being only a twopenny fare from the heart of the City. And we had a fireplace, a telephone, and an endless supply of hot water. 'Peter' welcomed us into her little flat during the Coronation week, and the arrangement was such a happy one, that we were pleased to make it our headquarters for the whole year. The front door of the little flat faced a tree-lined road, its main window looked out on to a pleasant grassed court where folk walked occasionally, and the muffin-man crossed on his ancient business.

Before reaching London we had learned with some excitement that a Coronation was to take place; but we had learned also that folk were paying ten, twenty, thirty, and more pounds for a seat for the day. Rene and I wanted a lot more than one day for our thirty pounds.

But on arrival we found that we had a Scottish friend—and one can't have too many of these. She had uncovered the fact that New Zealanders, by reason of their having come so far, were to have seats for fifteen shillings. Fifteen shillings! So she got us two.

The night before we went across London to a great rally of folk from all parts of the world; and because the 'bus routes were disorganized for the next day, we didn't get home until one o'clock in the morning.

When we did get home it was to find 'Peter' and a friend just in. They had been out to find a good place in which to stand. 'Well, it's one o'clock,' said one of them, 'I think we ought to get a few things ready.' So we put out our tickets and maps and weather-capes, we polished our shoes, we packed our sausage-rolls and sandwiches. And at two o'clock we went to bed.

At four o'clock, we got up ready to go. We knew the great event was not to happen for hours, but we knew also that it was wise to be early.

Many thousands, we soon discovered, had stayed up all night. One enterprising couple who had slept on the kerbside, were just getting up as we made our way. To a plane tree above their heads they had tied a Big Ben alarm clock.

Never shall we forget that day; all the public buildings and shops vying with one another in their decorations!

And then came the great procession—with all its colour and grace and pageantry; then the service in the Abbey—and we listened-in through the medium of loud-speakers artfully concealed among the trees. Never shall I forget the hush that settled on the crowd as the service came through.

A little wait—and there came the return procession— *the King seated beside the Queen.*

And then came the rain—and the poor dye ran out of our hats, and we looked the most sorry spectacle.

Somewhere about seven we reached home, tired—the most Scottish of us feeling that at any rate we'd had our fifteen-shillingsworth! To our surprise, 'Peter' and her friend were just in, and we found them sitting before the fire, drying-off and eating. 'Good gracious!' we exclaimed, 'are you still eating?' But, it transpired, they hadn't been eating at all. From a little after four in the morning, they'd stood at Hyde Park Corner in such a crowd, that they hadn't been able to get their hands up to their mouths; and they hadn't been able to use their handkerchiefs, they said; and they hadn't fainted—there just wasn't any room to faint. So they had kept on standing. And at seven o'clock in the evening, they had come home to eat their flattened sausage-rolls and sandwiches! And still, they said, it was worth it!

One of the most lasting memories of that day—and I think our King and Queen would be glad that it was so—was the love and loyalty shown the Queen Mother. The people of little Tristan da Cunha would have loved that.

I learned about Tristan da Cunha in the next days, and something about the Queen Mother.

Tristan da Cunha—a little island in the South Atlantic —is the loneliest island in the whole Empire. I used to think I'd like to go and live there—they haven't the telephone on! But they only get a mail once a year—so that isn't so good. And they haven't any trees—I couldn't live in a place without trees.

But one hundred and ninety people live on Tristan da Cunha; and only nine have ever seen the outside world. Their nearest neighbours are eighteen-hundred miles away. For all their hardships, they are a fit people—the only epidemic they know is an outbreak of colds after a ship has called. Death is due almost entirely to accident or old-age.

The thirty-five simple homes are huddled together within a quarter of a mile. The island resembles a great wheel, with a crater at the hub. Like spokes, great gulches radiate, and almost all round, perpendicular cliffs a thousand to two thousand feet, drop sheer into the sea.

Late in that same Coronation year, a scientific party landed on the island. The party was Norwegian, save for one Englishman. He went ashore with the first tiny craft that came out. 'The manipulation of the boat,' said he later, 'occupied all the crew's energy. Encouraged by a few friendly smiles I broke the long silence by explaining that I was an Englishman. . . . Someone eventually did speak, and it was the man at stroke.

' "How's the King and Queen?" he asked.

' "They're very well, thank you," the only Englishman present replied, making himself personally responsible for their Majesties' well-being.

' "Was they crowned?" was the next question.

' "Yes," was the simple answer.'

In March, it seemed, H.M.S. *Carlisle* had called, and the islanders had heard of the approaching Coronation of George the Sixth, and Queen Elizabeth.

But there were already strong links between the heart of the Empire and the loneliest little island within it. As the scientific party got ashore, they found their way that first night to a simple structure called the 'Parish Hall'. All round the walls were pictures from English magazines, and to their amazement, over the mantelshelf was a signed portrait of Queen Mary, the Queen Mother.

Actually it is of another personal link that I want to tell. In the busy weeks following on the Coronation, those seats for which people in London had been pleased to pay their ten, twenty, fifty pounds had to come down. Men with waggons and hammers and wrenches were called on, and in a very short time they had London looking like a disused timber-yard.

Now it happened that among those visiting London for the great Coronation, was the minister of Tristan da Cunha, the Reverend Harold Wilde. On the island, Mr. Wilde served as minister of the church, school-master, post-master—not a very strenuous job, of course, since they only got a mail once a year; but he was also registrar of births, deaths and marriages; and quite a lot of other importances.

One day, in those busy post-Coronation days, Mr. Wilde was out, and came upon the men ripping and tearing at the timbers. He noticed that they were dropping a lot of twisted six-inch nails. Forgetting for the moment where he was, he found himself thinking: 'They would be awfully handy if we had those back home.' And without further thought he began picking them up. Then he saw a few more, and picked them up, until presently he had all his pockets bulging with twisted nails.

At that, the foreman of works came down to have a little talk with him—and to learn who he was, and where he came from. And through the foreman of works, the story of this man from far-away Tristan da Cunha, and his nails, got to Queen Mary. At the time Queen Mary might have been forgiven if she had not thought of anyone but Queen Mary. But when she heard about it, she said: 'Tristan da Cunha! *He shall have some straight ones!*'

And so it was that as Mr. Wilde made his way back from London—the great throbbing heart of the Empire— to that little island—the loneliest island in the whole Empire—he took as a gift from the Queen Mother to the people of Tristan da Cunha, *two hundred-weight kegs of straight nails!*

What loving imagination! What out-reaching service! What motherly sense!

I wrote later to the secretary of the Society that sent Mr. Wilde to his island task, to check up on the story, and to ask permission to tell it—to me, one of the loveliest echoes of that great Coronation day.

XVIII

Does anyone with a little Scottish blood in her veins ever have enough Scottish history in her heart and head when she reaches Scotland? History may be only what one has called 'agreed fiction' until one is on the spot, then it becomes a great deal more.

We went north by 'bus, breaking the journey at York. It was a very pleasant way to travel. In 1763 there was only one stage coach in regular communication between Scotland and England. It left Edinburgh once a month, and took eighteen days to complete the journey. The roads were terrific. Arthur Young warned travellers in the north of England—before ever they got farther—against venturing their necks and limbs in that 'terrible country'.

But all that seemed to belong to the very far past that summer morning as we set off. The hedges slid pleasantly by, there were no ruts to endanger life and limb, and no highwaymen to waylay us. And there was enough of interest to keep us eager every inch of the way.

At Berwick we pulled up for our first Scottish tea. It was a characteristically liberal spread. There was no question of calling upon one to pick and choose—this sandwich and that cake—paying for each individually at the end, a wide-spread custom in English tea-shops that we found embarrassing when entertaining a friend. Scones and buns, and home-made cakes, were spread liberally on a large table, and we sat and made our tea at ease—a common charge covering our obligations.

Leaving Berwick by the Scotch Gate, crossing the railway, and keeping right at the fork of the road, we began to make the long, gradual rise—and to realize that we were in Scotland.

Edinburgh gave us bed that night, and enthralled us for the next few days. 'Every true Scotsman,' says Alexander Smith, 'believes Edinburgh to be the most picturesque city in the whole world.' We were in no mood to argue the point. We walked down Princes Street, we covered the ancient Royal Mile—every inch crowded with history; we came by way of Castle Hill into the Lawnmarket, past St. Giles Cathedral, into Canongate. We marked her colleges and churches and ancient monuments. 'Auld Reekie'—divided between the old city and the new, and set gloriously—was good to us. Sometimes her towers and spires were lost to view within the mists of earth that rose with magical effect, as much of her past was lost in the mists of tale and legend.

The Castle, set immovably upon its mighty rock, quickened the pulse. So ancient was it that history, as we counted history, ceased to count at all. The Britons had held it, the Romans, the Saxons, the Picts, in turn. Across the intervening gulf of spires and towers and chimney-tops, it looked sometimes unreal, but never at any time did it disappoint. It was exactly the kind of castle one felt a castle ought to be.

Climbing its steady roadway—up and up, the city spread out below us—we explored its precincts. It was a romantic and thrilling adventure—and a sobering one. The not-so-distant past came to us with reverent significance as we passed silently through its highest building, the Scottish National War Memorial, 'a coronach in stone'. There is nothing like it, set over its mighty upthrust of rock. Stone, bronze and stained-glass are used with such chaste and artistic discipline, that one is left with the sense of beautiful wholeness, and above all, with the splendour of ordinary human living, and the dignity of

PATTERNS OF A PASSING DAY
(Nelson)

sacrifice. To the right and left is the Hall of Honour, its walls occupied by regimental memorials, whilst its frieze bears the names of battle honours. Each Scottish regiment, raised in the home country or in the Dominions overseas, has its own memorial, and visitors can read, on the walls and in the Rolls of Honour, the numbers and names of those who served and fell. No one is forgotten—the inarticulate son who defended the rights of human life on the land, sea, or in the air; the woman at her task in the factory, the land-girl gathering in the harvest; the stretcher-bearer in the field, the nurse bending over the maimed and broken in hospital—all are remembered; the horses and donkeys—bearers of burdens—and the smallest of God's creatures, the carrier-pigeons, and the mice, 'the tunneller's friends'. From the Hall of Honour, one moves instinctively to the place of prayer and silence, The Shrine.

So everyone is remembered—remembered as he and she lived and served, neither 'glorified nor debased, but with a kind of dispassionate clarity'. One moves from that experience, for it is as much an experience as a place—straighter, and yet humbler, readier to serve a little more generously.

We paused a moment in Queen Mary's Bedroom—to hear again something of her ill-fated story, and to look down on the city from her window. In that tiny room, on 19th June, 1566, was born James the Sixth of Scotland and First of England.

We stood, with hushed hearts, in St. Giles Cathedral. We remembered, as all must remember with quickening pulse, the day when John Knox entered its pulpit, seeming feeble and weak but 'before he had don with his sermont was so actif and vigorus that he was lyk to ding that pulpit in blads and flie oot of it'.

We stood by his burial place in Parliament Square—an

SC—F

open space South of St. Giles, formerly the graveyard—marked by nothing more than a simple metal plate in the roadway, bearing his initials and a date.

We spent time in his house—the only pre-Reformation dwelling in Edinburgh, it is claimed, now preserving its original architectural features.

Three things interested me specially in that house—the candle, first, that burns at both ends, that I had heard about every time my family and friends had decided I was crowding too much into my days and nights. The candle that burned at both ends, I discovered, was strictly a flexible taper, held in a kind of metal rush-light holder. By bending the taper and lighting both ends at once, the light of the 'candle' of course, could be doubled, but the life of the 'candle' reduced by half. There was something appealing, generous, reckless about it. Edna St. Vincent Millay's words seemed the only adequate comment, and I quoted them with a twinkle, as many a time before:

> *My candle burns at both ends,*
> *It will not last the night,*
> *But ah, my friends,*
> *And oh, my foes,*
> *It gives a lovely light.*

Another simple thing of interest was the tirling-pin. Is there a child anywhere who has not at some time been put to bed with

> *Wee Willie Winkie rinning thro' the town,*
> *Upstairs and downstairs in his nicht gown,*
> Tirlin' *at the window,* crying at the lock:
> '*Are the weens in their beds, for it's now ten o'clock?*'

The tirling-pin proved to be a piece of metal with rough teeth along its edge, its ends fixed a few inches apart, into

158

the door jamb, raised a little above the surface of the wood. Hanging enclosed within it, was a metal ring that one held firmly and ran up and down the notched metal. It made a sound like a stick along a corrugated wall. Nowhere else in Scotland did we happen upon a tirling-pin. Brass-knockers and press-bells seemed to have won the day.

Another interesting link with the past was the door-nail. I had heard the expression 'Dead as a door-nail', but it had never made much impression on me. Now it came alive—if anything as dead as a door-nail could be said to come alive. Even Dickens had missed the significance of the door-nail. Speaking of Old Marley in *A Christmas Carol* he had given himself away by saying: 'Old Marley was as dead as a door-nail. Mind, I don't mean to say that I know, of my own knowledge, what there is particularly dead about a door-nail. I might have been inclined, myself, to regard a coffin-nail as the deadest piece of iron-mongery in the trade. . . .' Now, I had out-distanced Dickens. Here to 'my own knowledge' was a door-nail. Against a metal boss, could be lifted and let drop a chunk of iron, with a hammer head, fixed into the oaken door. And the noise it made was the deadest of dead sounds.

So I came from John Knox's house with three pleasant, unexpected pieces of information, apart from a great deal of history and legend about the great man himself.

But the tablet of Jenny Geddes, near the gate entering the Moray Aisle, seemed the most human thing. In St. Giles, on Sunday, 23rd July, 1637, the famous incident took place. Charles the First had decreed that the English Church service should be read in every parish church in Scotland, and as Dean Hannay in St. Giles rose to give out the collect for the day, a kail-wife, Jenny Geddes, incensed, took up her stool and flung it at his head, with the result that a thorough-going riot ensued. 'Constant oral tradition,' says practical Jenny's tablet, 'affirms that near this spot a brave Scottish woman, Janet Geddes, on the 23rd July 1637, struck the first blow in the great struggle for freedom of conscience, which after a conflict of half a century ended in the establishment of civil and religious liberty.' Near by is a tablet to the Dean: 'To James Hannay, D.D., Dean of this Cathedral, 1634--49. He was the first and the last who read the service book in this church. This memorial is erected in happier times by his descendant.'

In the Church of Scotland Assembly Hall, and in the quiet graveyard of Greyfriars where age and moss had obliterated the wording from the stones, we found it impossible to forget a scene that men and women of Scotland never forget, when crowded round a *thruchstane* tomb— a flat grave-stone, which served as a table—a company of solemn men and women signed the National Covenant, and pledged themselves to the Presbyterian form of worship, one after another opening a vein in an arm to sign the documents in life blood.

But many of these great events were significant far beyond Edinburgh. We found them echoed in Glasgow, in the Highlands, and the lonely Isles of the Hebrides.

Glasgow welcomed us into the heart of Scottish hospitality. Our friends took us round their ancient and vigorous city, and planned for us a trip down the Clyde to the lovely Isle of Arran, and a walking trip through the Trossacks.

Loch Katrine was a name known to us from childhood, but more as a legend than a real place. But as we humped our haversacks, and grasped our stout sticks, it became a reality for ever. Beyond Callander, where we left the train, the Trossacks became for us an experience. At the centre was a white winding road disappearing ever over a ridge

160

of hills to some remote, unseen destination—an experience of mauves and purples, of water-side roads and mountains, of sun, and ancient winds ceaselessly remembering ancient things.

'Given the right companion,' says the author of *Heather Track and High Road*, 'I see no reason in the world why a journey should not be crammed with memorable things.'

From Glasgow we went north, past Stirling Castle, to Oban, and from Oban to Iona.

There are certain spots in this world that remain for ever in one's memory because of their pristine loveliness. Such for me is the ancient island of Iona. So small and modest is the island itself, set in the midst of the Western Isles that one who has not paused to learn the secret of its spell, may well wonder at its hold upon so many hearts.

Its shores are washed unceasingly by the free Atlantic seas. On a clear summer day, and particularly when the wind is in the north, its beauty is idyllic. The blue sky over all may be lightly veiled with soft cirrus clouds, the sea glistening green as an opal, barred at a distance with vivid blue and purple. Over all is a sense of peace, enriched by the granite cliffs of Mull across the Sound, and the great mountains beyond, with their deep blue purple shadows.

But it is not its absence of trees, or its simple profusion of flowers that one remembers after one has come back to a more prosaic world, to walk a little more softly ever afterwards. The secret lies farther to seek, in the realm of the spirit.

Thirteen hundred years ago, on the last day of his life, St. Columba ascended the little hill overlooking the monastery, and raising his eyes for the last time, blessed this island of his adoption: 'Unto this place, small and mean though it be, great honour shall yet be paid not only by the kings and peoples of the Scots, but by the rulers of barbarous and distant nations with their people. Thy saints also, of other churches, shall regard it with no common reverence.'

And so it has come to be.

Choosing twelve followers in A.D. 563 as his Master had done before him, St. Columba left his beloved Ireland, in a frail coracle of wicker and hides. Landing first on another island (according to tradition) he discovered that his beloved Ireland was still in sight. Deciding that he could not fully serve with its irresistible pull upon his affections, he set sail, and so came to Iona. Other and more practical considerations may have had a place in his selection of Iona. Islands had a special attraction for the founders of the early Celtic Church. Though their vessels were small and frail, the sea was the easiest highway.

That, we knew, was all a very long time ago. Columba had served on Iona, and died an old man, by the year St. Augustine came to England, in A.D. 597.

There is a lovely story told of his birth. Descended from the royal house, he was born in a wild, mountainous part of Donegal. Columba's mother, Eithne, was of royal blood. It is said that before her son was born, she dreamed that an angel stood beside her, and offered her a robe of exquisite beauty. But scarcely had she reached out for it, than the angel took it and spread it out, till it covered 'mountain and lough and forest, reaching even to Scotland'. By this sign, she knew that her son was to be among the chosen ones of God's service; so his early education was accordingly directed.

The lads of the neighbourhood who joined him coming from the cell in which he read his psalms, called him by the lovely name, Columcille—Colum of the cell or church. Columba, the name by which we know him to-day, is the Latin form of Colum.

He might have sat upon the throne of Erin had he not abandoned it for the service of Christ; but he did choose the service of Christ, and history was changed. In a dark age, Iona became a centre of Christian living. He learned the language, and with his followers tilled the soil, and filled the days with prayer and study. Above all, the church on Iona became a missionary church. From the little island eager men crossed to England, and even to Europe. And in time, the powerful King of the Picts, 'the race which had withstood the legions of Rome herself,' succumbed to these brothers in Christ.

So Columba lived, and so he died. And though to-day there remains no single trace of the buildings erected in his time he lies in the little opal island, interred in a simple grave, in the manner of his time. On his isle are also buried forty-eight crowned kings of ancient Scotland, four of Ireland, and seven of Norway, and many princes, chiefs and ecclesiastics of Celtic Scotland.

But it is not death that pervades Iona—it is Life. Many of the old buildings dating from the thirteenth century are being restored, and even within the ruined walls of the Nunnery is a garden of unimaginable beauty. I have never seen anything more like an opal for colour than the natural stone walls, and the pinks and mauves and blues of the lupins clustered within. It is a living thing.

And life of another kind came to the island in 1938, when the Iona Community was founded by the Rev. Dr. George Macleod, of the Church of Scotland. An integral part of the work of those who are members of the Community for the term of two years, is the rebuilding of the abbey in the summer months; during the winter they go off in pairs to work out the vision of Iona in the great crowded industrial centres and parishes of Scotland. The

163

Community believes that 'the primary problem before mankind is how to plan society, and at the same time preserve the rights of the individual'—and in the Christian Church, wedded again to common life, it finds the key to this world problem.

So the past and the present mingle inextricably on Iona.

We can learn much from the Saint's unquestioning faith and service—we can learn something also from one of his foibles. There exists an old Gaelic proverb expressing the tradition that he would suffer to remain on the isle neither a cow nor a woman:

> *Far am bi bo, bithidh bean;*
> *'S far am bi bean, bithidh mallachadh.*

'Where there is a cow, a woman will be; and where there is a woman there will be mischief.'

But nothing, of course, is so simple as that. Columba had fallen into the error pathetically widespread in our day—*the error of over-simplification.* 'Only let me have an extra pound in my pay-envelope,' says one, 'and all will be well.' It won't. 'Only let us have one language that the nations in conference can understand one another, and all will be well.' It won't! None of these things alone is the secret of the good life. 'Attempts are sometimes made to define the spirit of the age in a single phrase—to call it, for example, "an age of doubt," "an age of rationalism," "an age of revolt,"' says Dr. J. S. Stewart, a son of Scotland. '*The reality cannot be thus simplified.* We have to reckon with a mental and spiritual climate of the most baffling contradictions.' We have to take account of something wrong at the heart of things—and we have no choice, however modern we are, we must call that something 'sin'.

It is a conviction as ancient as the ancient faith of Scotland—reaching up to God, and deep down into human hearts. And it is not out of place that one's love of Scotland, with its castles and kings and kirks, should end on this theological note. Nothing so surely matches the spirit of this ancient and energetic people.

XIX

WITH haversacks, sticks and sturdy tramping shoes we explored the Highlands, from a little crofter's cottage; we climbed into a pass of the Cairngorms; we crossed to Skye, where the very name of the Coolins is music to the ears; back through the Highlands to Inverness, where the sun goes down with a flood of glory; and down to Gala-shiels, Selkirk, Abbotsford, Melrose, Dryburgh—names, every one of them, crammed with history and instinct with poetry. Amid the graceful loveliness of those ancient stones, it was not hard to hear

> *. . . sounds of insult, shame and wrong,*
> *And trumpets blown for wars. . . .*

We made our leisurely way down to the English Lakes. In the morning the sun looked into our eyes, and in the evening went down into a great quietness, leaving something of eternal peace in our hearts.

> *Ah! then was it all spring weather?*
> *Nay, but we were young, and together.*

We stayed in youth hostels, beginning the day with cooking around the open fire. Meals over, haversacks packed, and our share of tidying-up done, we set out for long heathery scrambly tramps.

The Youth Hostel Association of Great Britain had been only seven years established, though there had been for some years hostels of a similar character in European countries.

Hostels varied greatly we found—that was part of their charm. Some were old castles with a romantic history,

166

some weavers' cottages, thatched and supported with great oaken beams; others were ancient manor houses; some had been built for the purpose. Despite the differences, there were a number of features in common. Each provided accommodation for both men and women—dormitories, common-room, washing and simple cooking facilities. Provided also were bunks—mattresses, blankets and pillows. Each wayfarer was obliged to carry or hire the special hostel sheet—fashioned like an official envelope, with a flap in front that completely covered the blankets, and a pocket at the back, into which a pillow could be fitted.

Some hostels offered a hot meal for a small sum. All were closed during the middle of the day, so that there was no opportunity for lazy folk to loiter. At the day's end we turned in, signed our names on a register and greeted strangers with a 'hail-fellow-well-met', sharing our adventures of the day.

'I am told there are some people who do not care for maps,' said R.L.S. 'I find it hard to believe.' He would have been the more at a loss to explain such lack of spirit could he have spent an evening with a youth-hostel map; for in addition to the usual 'hairy caterpillars' for mountains, and wiggly blue lines for rivers and streams, were small well-placed triangles for hostels. It was a game to ponder over a map, and space out one's sleeping places.

The term 'youth' seemed to embrace all who were youthful enough to make a journey under youth-hostel conditions. The youngest wayfarer we met was a self-conscious youth of fourteen who had never before stayed away from home, and the oldest was a widowed school-master of seventy odd, making a journey on a bicycle in the first days of his loneliness. It was charming to watch the developing friendship and interdependence of those two.

Another happy feature of hostel life was the total

167

absence of any national barrier. Relaxed, after an evening meal, limb weary, kissed by sun and wind, we spent happy hours with fellow-members who, for all their differences, loved passionately the things we loved.

It seemed an odd thing to reflect that before the nineteenth century, walking for pleasure was rare in England. Apart from being considered unsafe, it was counted an eccentric idea. When Shelley planned a walking tour, it was through France, since in England, said he, 'it would involve continual insult and impertinence'. Hazlitt and Lamb were a little more daring.

In time, the bicycle presented a new factor, and lovers of the countryside were able to go farther afield. 'Cads on casters' they were called, but that did not deter real country-lovers. By degrees, some of them learned to combine the pleasures of walking and cycling, on what they called 'walcling tours'—cycling down hill, and toilfully pushing up where riding was impossible.

In their way, members of the Youth Hostel Association combine these two pleasant ways of travel to-day, since the hostels are open only to walkers and cyclists—those who can afford to whisk themselves about by car, must pass by this simple fellowship.

So we came again to London, our first love, and to 'Peter's' little flat. Sometimes we shared our meal with her at the day's end, sometimes she shared with us. Sometimes we sat over the fire, sharing her passion for Shakespeare; sometimes we set off together to visit some old, little-known part of London, or to hunt for treasure in the second-hand bookshops in Charing Cross Road.

Springtime coaxed us across to Holland; summer took us to Paris. In between, we visited Oxford, its spires 'unearthly in their beauty, set in the misty blue of early May'; we motored through the Wye Valley; we meandered in Shakespeare's lovely Warwickshire; we found our way to Milton's cottage, to Stoke Poges, where Gray wrote his 'Elegy Written in a Country Churchyard'; to Jordans, with its old Quaker Meeting-house and great gift of peace.

> *Some things can be logged, like dates;*
> *The points of interest on the route,*
> *The best hotels, the famous heroes with their tragic fates,*
> *The types of landscapes and the ruined towers:*
> *But guide-books cannot tell you all the rest.*

No one can log the joy that meets one unexpectedly, the sunlight on an old wall, the conversation by the way, the taste of strange food.

In the colourful autumn we crossed again to the Continent—to Belgium, Germany, Switzerland, Austria.

'Travaile, in the younger sort,' said Francis Bacon, 'is a part of education; in the elder, a part of experience.' We were of the 'younger sort', but there were times when we remembered that 'travaile' and 'travel' were once one and the same. In some of our most strenuous days in ancient cities, we almost joined them together again. 'The things to be seene and observed,' said Bacon, 'are the churches, and monasteries with the monuments which are therein extant; the walls and fortifications of cities and townes; and so the havens and harbours: antiquities, and ruins: libraries, colledges, disputations and lectures, where any are: armories, arsenals, magazines, burses: warehouses: exercises of souldiers, and the like: treasures of jewels, and robes: cabinets, and rareties: and to conclude, whatsoever is memorable in the places where they goe.'

At times our travel was as packed as Bacon's list, but the lasting delight lay in the more leisurely ways, in the people we met, and in the experiences that quickened our spirits.

The two of us once travelled in a third-class French railway-carriage—the sort of thing you only do once.

For hours we were shut in our crowded carriage, small and overheated. Condensation trickled down the windows, and nobody seemed to be able to open them, or to turn off the heat. At one place we took on an old gentleman with a bag of shell-fish—and the salt water ran all over the floor. A station or two farther on we took on an old gentleman with a very powerful pipe—a very powerful pipe. Already, a tired mother tried to pacify a little baby but it whimpered and whimpered its unhappiness, mingling with the miserable heat of the carriage, the unpleasantness of the shell-fish, and the stench of the powerful pipe.

My friend and I were as tired as any; and we had not heard a word of English in days.

Then for some reason, our train pulled into a wayside station—nobody knew why, nobody knew when we would go on again.

In the next carriage were some lads going to a camp up in the hills. As the wait became irksome they dragged from their camp gear a gramophone and some records. It was one of those little gramophones—those very little gramophones with loud needles! And record after record ripped its way through the thick atmosphere of our carriage.

Then quite suddenly, everything was changed—for one weary passenger at anyrate. For into that place poured the loveliest, richest tones heard in years—*the first English in days*—Dame Clara Butt singing that glorious hymn of Henry Lyte's 'Abide with me!'

Those lovely rich tones! Those lovely rich words! Never shall I forget that experience! For Christ was in that place—though I was far from home, among strangers, and in war-weary Europe.

I must have heard that hymn before a thousand times, but never as then, when I overheard it.

I confess it now. Of course, I ought never to have forgotten the Emmaus Road, and those other weary travellers. I ought never to have forgotten the work of the Risen Christ. But how easily one forgets!

XX

OVER our favourite fireplace at home we have a picture of Beethoven. A pastel in soft browns and greens, it shows him with hair windswept, and jaw set as he walks with his thoughts.

'Is that Beethoven?' exclaimed a friend of years, when some reference was made to the picture. 'I always thought that was Napoleon!' Why she imagined we would want to enshrine the memory of Napoleon, I can't think; but we have a life-long and growing reason for remembering that great gusty genius who walked in the storm.

Neither Rene nor I will ever forget the late afternoon when we came to Bonn, on the banks of the Rhine. We had been several weeks in Germany. We had gone down the river from Cologne to Coblenz, and on to Wiesbaden, Frankfurt, Nuremberg, Munich, Oberammergau in the Bavarian Alps, into Austraia and across to Switzerland, and up through Frieberg and the Black Forest, Baden-Baden, Heidelberg (the old university town), Worms (the town of Martin Luther), Kreuznach, Bingen on the Rhine (bringing back memories of school, and a poem of that name), on by boat up the famous stretch of the river barons, the bank studded with old castles, to Boppard, Cochem, Adenau, Altenahr, Godesberg, and so to Cologne.

Our minds were crowded with pictures. Down the Moselle Valley it had been harvest-time, and we had stopped at the wayside vineyards and taken part in the in-gathering of grapes. At Oberammergau we had lunched and talked with the wood carvers of the village, who at the season appointed give themselves with wonderful devotion to the presentation of the Passion Play. We had crossed the Danube, though it was scarcely the 'Blue Danube' that we had been led to expect; we had spent an hour enthralled at the old clockmaker's museum in the forest. Castles innumerable, old city walls, winding roads and their straggling traffic of peasants with their quaint home-made vehicles had been part of the scene. We had heard opera in Wiesbaden, observed en route the smoking factories, and the orderly, feverish activity in Munich, when Mussolini had come to open a great road of some thousands of miles without a corner or a bend. All these things and more were in our minds. And then we came to Bonn.

It was late in the day, and there was some thought of our being refused admission. But when we knocked, the door was opened by an elderly gentleman, although he and his family were at their evening meal. We told him who we were, and where we had come from, emphasizing the fact that we were lovers of Beethoven.

That was the magic key that gave us open sesame, as well it might. We were taken through the great doors into the pleasant, irregular little garden and into that part of the house where are assembled memories and records of the great life that began there. To-day, that birthplace under the eaves is bare, save for a fine bust of Beethoven, with a laurel wreath at its base. In its plainness and severity it is very impressive, but there is much else to see in that old house. Beethoven's first piano is there—and his last piano. And the original manuscripts of the 'Moonlight Sonata' and other famous works, and the announcement of his first public concert, given when he was a child.

Beethoven was fortunate that his father was a lover of music, but he was greatly to be pitied that he was also a drunkard. He did little to support the family, and by the

time the lad was twelve, he was earning his living as a
'cymbalist', a harpsichord player, in a theatre orchestra.
He was seventeen before his great wish to go to Vienna
came true. Even then, he was unable to stay long. Word
reached him that his mother was dying, and he had to
hurry back. But he was in Vienna long enough to make
one very important friend, Mozart, then about thirty
years of age. He gave the young visitor lessons that were
invaluable. Later he also had lessons from Haydn.

He had a few good friends in Bonn. A family called
Von Bruening was very good to him. Count Waldstein
was another good friend, and Beethoven was moved to
dedicate to him in later years, his 'Waldstein Sonata'.

He settled in Vienna, and there he remained for the
greater part of his life. He was a warm-hearted, generous
man, loving the country of woods and fields. One of his
most famous works was the 'Pastoral Symphony', captur-
ing something of the calm of the countryside, the songs of
the birds, the music of the brooks. Nature gave him inspiration too, in her more boisterous moods, and helped
him in some of the great difficulties he had to face.

One of the most moving things in that old house in Bonn
that offers so much was a set of ear-trumpets. The first was
quite small, but as deafness intensified, the trumpets
increased in size, in a futile and pathetic effort to hear his
own music. As we stood looking at them, it seemed one of
the saddest things in the world that a master-musician
might not hear his own music. He also had a piano made
with extra pedals, but it was all of no avail.

Of course, Beethoven was not an easy man to live with.
But during his period of total deafness he composed some
of the most marvellous music of the world, which will be
listened to as long as men have ears, and his memory will
be kept green in that old house in Bonn.

During the war I wondered what fate had befallen that

old house. To my great joy, I have learned that it still stands. Almost every other building in the narrow street was either badly damaged or wrecked. How then did Beethoven's house escape? The answer is in the devotion of its old caretaker, who for years has lived for Beethoven. And for Beethoven he risked danger to life and limb when a big fire-bomb raid was made on the town. Most of the people of Bonn had evacuated to safer places across the river, but the old caretaker stayed at his post, and put out the incendiaries that must have destroyed for ever his precious house and museum.

In the main square of Bonn, is a monument to the master-musician. And as I look at our pastel of Beethoven walking in the storm, my thoughts go back to the soft autumn evening when we came to his house in Bonn, and I rejoice that war has not destroyed his monument nor his house. Nothing, I know, can ever destroy his music.

XXI

One morning outside 'Peter's' London flat we waited for a Number 77 'bus while two women with shopping-baskets stood by. We could hardly help overhearing their conversation. One had a tale of woe, of how insult had been heaped upon her.

'And what did you do?' asked the other.

'I just stood upon my dignity,' came the thin-lipped reply.

Before we could return that evening by the 77 'bus, the subject of dignity had taken on a new significance: we had shared a cup of tea with Mrs. Hugh Price Hughes.

The name of the Rev. Hugh Price Hughes was one we had known always. A minister of the Methodist Church, and son of a minister of the Church, he was referred to as 'the greatest gift to his Church since Wesley'. A big man —physically, mentally, spiritually—councils and municipalities became more humane under pressure from Hugh Price Hughes. W. T. Stead likened him to 'a day of Judgement in trousers' where social injustice was concerned. Founder and Superintendent of the West London Mission, minister, lecturer and editor of a church paper, he wore himself out.

It was a memorable experience to take tea with his widow, Katherine Price Hughes—eighty and a bit, with a lifetime of service to London behind her. (She lived to the great age of ninety-four, and died only in 1948.)

I had long known of her outstanding gifts—her platform ability, her administrative genius in the Sisterhood, her distinctive contribution to the Church, her never-failing sense of humour. And I had seen her up in her pew on the Sunday—a little greying woman, oldish, roundish, with quizzical eyes, and good characterful mouth. I had thought what an enriching thing it would be to take a cup of tea with her; and before I could do anything about it, the mail brought me an invitation to visit her on the second day of the New Year.

Imagine then my double pleasure and surprise when on the *first* day of the New Year, I opened my newspaper to find there her picture, among others. She had been given an honour by the King—was named in the New Year's Honours List!

So my first thought, on being received next day, was to congratulate her on the honour which had come to her. I shall never forget that moment, as she stood there in her little tea-apron. 'Well, my dear,' said she very simply, 'I never thought anything like this would happen to me. I'm not properly used to it yet. When the news first came, I didn't know what to do about it. To tell you the truth, I just had to take a couple of aspirins, and go and lie down.' (Which I thought a lovely way to receive an honour from the King). 'I just felt,' she added, 'like a common barn-door fowl that had somehow taken on peacock's feathers, and really you know, they don't suit me.'

One of the first things she had noticed, as we had done, was that her picture was alongside that of Gracie Fields, who had received an honour for quite a different thing. At once this little old lady had gone down and sent off a message of congratulation to Gracie. Turning to me, she said: 'You know, I've been all my life here bucking them up—giving them old clothes, and soup, and things to think about—all my life I've been bucking them up.' And after a minute's thought: 'And she's been doing the same. Of course, I couldn't do it in her way.'

'No,' I added, 'and not many of us could, either. But

then she couldn't have done it in your way, and have kept it up all these years.'

No wonder that, as we made our way back by the 77 'bus, it was with a new understanding of dignity—*of dignity and humility*. We had seen the two so closely related in the person of our little old hostess. Emerson had spoken of those 'who forget themselves into immortality'. Similarly, it seemed, there were people who forgot themselves into dignity. Dignity was not really for standing on.

> *True dignity abides with her alone*
> *Who, in the silent hour of inward thought*
> *Can still respect, can still revere herself*
> *In lowliness of heart.*

Dick Sheppard was another servant of London, whom I had long known by name, who understood dignity. And when he 'fell on death' quietly as he sat alone at his desk, on that last morning of October, great London paused to remember its debt. *Dick Sheppard forgot himself.* He loved people—that was the greatest thing about him—unless it was that, above all, he loved his Lord.

London knew him first when he came to St. Martin-in-the-Fields. The old church stood no longer in the fields, but in the midst of great banks and offices, its graceful spire upreaching to heaven like the secret aspirations of men. Its feet were set on the edge of 'the never-ceasing torrents of the Strand'. Dick Sheppard early decided that its doors should never be shut. War-weary men waiting for trains, were welcomed during the first World War; and street-weary people, and homeless, were welcomed into the peace and warmth of the crypt, when war was at an end. When the new miracle of wireless came to London, Dick Sheppard's church was the first to broadcast.

Through strenuous years, thousands of worshippers

178

found what they needed at St. Martin's, and it became not at all uncommon to have to stand in a queue.

In time, Dick Sheppard—the Rev. H. R. L. Sheppard, Vicar of St. Martin-in-the-Fields, friend of all—was made Chaplain to the King. Then with the passing of the years, he became Dean of Canterbury Cathedral, that lovely shrine where faith goes down to its roots. Then he was made Canon of St. Paul's, upraising its cross over the human joys and tears of London. Hating war, he next dreamed and established the Peace Pledge Union; and eight days before his service on earth was finished, the students of Glasgow University elected him Lord Rector.

When the news went out that Dick Sheppard was dead, those closest to him were shocked, and great London most of all.

His body was brought into the old church, that those who loved him might do him honour. And all that morning, and afternoon and evening they came, thousands of men and women who counted life a little gayer, and more purposeful, because Dick Sheppard had passed that way. I shall not soon forget that reverent filing company. It was the sort of congregation our Lord would have loved. There were the shy, ill-clad men and women of the streets who slept in the crypt, down-and-outs; there were the King's men in their immaculate uniforms; and near them, ordinary mortals like ourselves; and as if life had suddenly lost all its differences, the high dignitaries of the Church; and old ladies in their shawls, who sold flowers outside Charing Cross; and a little old man with a stick and a cork leg who sold jumping celluloid dolls off some stone steps not far away.

Two or three days later, I was again on the 77 'bus, and heard two old men talking. And what they said moved me to write it down on the back of my bus-ticket. Said one, 'Awful sad 'bout poor Dick Sheppard, ain't it?' 'Don't you poor 'im,' replied the other. ''E's all right. God'll be right glad to 'ave 'im and all.' And that I knew to be one of the loveliest tributes ever paid to Dick Sheppard—that he would be as much at home in Heaven as he had been on earth.

It was whilst I was in London that I came on a new understanding of '*the dignity of Death*'. One day with hushed heart, I stood in Westminster Abbey, to represent the family, at the funeral of a New Zealander, Ernest Rutherford—Lord Rutherford of Nelson, O.M., F.R.S., Cavendish Professor of Experimental Physics in the University of Cambridge. He had visited our home in Nelson, and I had planned to visit him in Cambridge. But on our return from the Continent in the autumn, we were faced as we landed with a newspaper hoarding bearing the words: 'Greatest British Scientist dead.'

In Westminster Abbey, it seemed at first a far cry from that sacred spot to a little shingle-roofed cottage near my home in Nelson. And yet, of course, it was not. 'With the death of Rutherford,' one said, 'a great epoch in science came to an end—Rutherford was the Newton of the atom.' Lord Baldwin had said of him: 'His refreshing personality, his dauntless spirit, the merry twinkle of his eye, the exuberance of his ever-youthful enthusiasm . . . one can only say he was a man, a peer among men: he was Rutherford.'

And now he was dead.

As the Elegy hushed all hearts, followed by the Chorale Preludes of Bach, I remembered these things, and what my father had told me of his early beginnings. Fame had come to him, but he had not been slow to honour his parents, humble people and true. His father had come out from Scotland as a lad; his mother had been one who valued education for her children. My father knew his cousin well in those early days. He remembered him saying that but for gaining a scholarship to Nelson College, he might have been a farmer, and never realized his special gifts.

By steps Ernest got to Cambridge, to McGill, to Manchester, and back to Cambridge—to the direction of a physical laboratory for nearly forty years. And here for a moment Time seemed to stop.

The opening sentences in the noble Service of Burial rose to high Heaven, to Dr. Croft's music: 'I am the Resurrection and the Life, saith the Lord: he that believeth in Me, though he were dead, yet shall he live; and whosoever liveth and believeth in Me shall never die.'

As hymns, prayers and readings proceeded, and the procession moved slowly to the grave-side, I realized in a new way the meaning of 'the dignity of Death'. I heard in a new way the ancient words! 'In the midst of life we are in death: of whom may we seek for succour, but of Thee, O Lord Who for our sins art justly displeased? Yet, O Lord God most holy, merciful Saviour, deliver us not into the bitter pains of eternal death. Thou knowest, Lord, the secrets of our hearts: shut not Thy merciful ears to our prayers; but spare us, Lord most holy, O God most mighty, O holy and merciful Saviour. . . .'

So the day closed, and we turned with humble hearts, from the quiet resting-place of 'New Zealand's greatest son'—by the immortal Sir Isaac Newton.

XXII

I was in London when my second book—the first with an English publisher—came out. It was a modest enough book, following the style of the first—a collection of letters brought together in the belief that life is all of a piece—religion and literature, friendship, travel, common everyday affairs, and because God saw that we should never achieve much without it, humour also. Publishers and reviewers were kind. The first word I saw in print, said of it: 'The author of this delightful book has culture, a clear sense of beauty, and a deep spiritual understanding. . . .'

I shall never forget when I first saw a pile of my books in a shop window. Nothing short of 'all the King's horses and all the King's men' could have dragged me to gaze into that window again, until I was sure that its display had been changed. Those who have not written a book, and seen a little bit of their soul between two covers—offered alike to friend, foe and fool—will not understand. There is no going back; for better or worse, it is done. There is no rapture like it—and no shyness.

In that moment I recalled Dickens's confession when he ventured into authorship. He had dropped a few sketches anonymously into a publisher's letter-box. Only later did he know their fate when he bought a monthly magazine and saw his work in print. He had 'to turn into Westminster Hall for half an hour, because,' said he, 'my eyes were so dimmed with joy and pride that they could not bear the street, and were not fit to be seen there'. Every writer ever since, I believe, has entered into something of that experience.

When a writer is required to write or speak about himself, it seems almost to be taken for granted that he will have something to tell of early struggles. How did he contrive to begin—to set down in twenty-six stubborn letters what was in his heart, to lay hold of thoughts lighter than gossamer, lovelier and more fleet? And how did he get time to write—though E. Arnot Robertson has suggested that it is a 'little like asking how ever he found the leisure to cut his first tooth, or by what means an epileptic gets a minute to spare in which to have a fit; writing, like these things, just happens to the born writer, and takes whatever time it wants.' And there are other questions: how did he manage to penetrate editorial reluctance? Did he have to send out his manuscript again and again? Did he have to say with Jean Paul, in the long, care-filled meanwhile, 'to a great height shall the business of hungering go'?

I was more than usually fortunate in this respect—fortunate in the success attending my first book, fortunate in knowing very well the people for whom I wrote, fortunate most of all perhaps, in having my work accepted, and immediately, by the Epworth Press. An hour after my arrival in London, I was wending my way to City Road, where the great Press raises its storied head, a stone's throw from the spot where John Wesley established it two hundred years ago.

That day, as a copy of my book was placed into my hand, I could not know what adventures we should have together. Nor that the Rev. Edgar C. Barton, the book steward, was to establish himself my good friend.

It has always been customary to wail against the sins of publishers. A century before Wesley established the press that was to bear the name of his birthplace—Epworth—there appeared in *The Schollers Purgatory* an irate passage headed: 'Publisher, a Bad One.' 'He prayseth no books'—the old wail began, 'but what sells well, and that must be his own Coppy too, or els he will have some flirt with it: No matter, though there be no cause: For, he knowes he shall not be questioned for what hee sayes, or if he be, his impudence is enough to outface it. What he beleeves is prepared for him in the next world, I know not. If he gett any written Coppy into his powre, it shall be contrived and named also, according to his owne pleasure: which is the reason so many good Bookes come forth imperfect, with such foolish titles.'

Whatever the sins of publishers to-day, I feel certain they are not all on the one side.

Most authors take themselves seriously—which is to be expected. But mischief occurs when we take ourselves too seriously. Some setting an artistic pose favour beads—large arty beads; others, of the opposite sex, beards—carefully cultivated beards. But surely the test of a writer's worth is in what he writes; if he writes well he will not need to draw attention to his existence by eccentric behaviour. I am all for normality.

It may be true that a writer is more sensitive to the tides of life than most; it is true that transference of heart and mind to paper is a wondrous business; it is also true that a writer must pay his rent and keep himself nourished. The baker who supplies his 'unbuttered bread' may be, in at least two ways, more fortunate. Says Phyllis Bottome: 'The difference between the baker and the artist—here meaning author—is that the artist is more involved in his work. Even if the baker is a very good baker, there is less of him in his loaf than there is of the artist in his work of art. Both should be skilled workmen, and both supply the public with what it needs, but whereas the baker more or less mechanically supplies an immediate want, the artist, by his own growth, and with himself as material, has to supply a less immediate want. He has even to train his audience to realize their need of his produce, whereas nature settles the need of the baker's audience.'

But a writer becomes distracted, or what is only a little less distressing, a figure of fun, when he becomes over-serious. Sometimes it shows itself in a fear that inspiration has ceased. Even Dickens had his moments. In a letter to a friend, he poured out: 'I have not written a single slip. My wretchedness is inconceivable. . . . How I work, how I walk, how I shut myself up. . . . How I settle to nothing.' And Thackeray, before settling to '*The New-comes*', wrote 'Yesterday I sat for six hours and could do no work. . . . My groans were heartrending, and my sufferings immense.' In Mrs. Atherton's over-seriousness there is room for a wry smile, but it is our smile, not hers. Unable to get on with a novel that she had promised, having exhausted all human means, this good soul sought out the shrine of Bonsecours, and addressed a desperate prayer to the Almighty, beginning: 'Now, look here!'

The question is: ought a writer to work, to wait, or to walk up and down? Which way does inspiration come? A. A. Milne jibes at writers who sit waiting to be miraculously inspired. He imagines one such saying to his wife at breakfast, 'My dear, if I am not inspired by eleven o'clock I shall want the car.' Milne—with a body of good work to show, wise and sweetly reasonable, is on the side of those who work, who apply themselves to thorough preparation, who discipline their moods and whims to certain regular periods of application. And if I may say so, I am on the side of Milne. Believe in inspiration? Of course, but who shall say how it comes? 'The wind bloweth where it listeth.'

If we writers are to be saved from taking ourselves too seriously, I think we must realize that a book is only half our effort—the other half belongs to the reader. Clemence

Dane has put it plainly for us '*The reader and writer are one flesh*, and of their union the living book is born.'

Unhappily, the reader does not always realize this. He takes up a book—the precious outpouring of some author's soul—and turns on the wireless, as a kind of background interest; he reads the reviews—some of them written by men as fallible as himself—to make up his mind before ever he turns a page; or he begins his reading with a little snippit in the middle of the book, or worse, with the last pages, to 'see what the hero dies of', or to 'to see if she got him in the end.' He is liable to welcome most those books that confirm his own opinions, to ask of fiction that it shall be true, of poetry that it shall be false, of biography that it shall be flattering.

Now, of course, that isn't playing the game.

If the average reader were to take himself a little more seriously, perhaps the poor author need not take himself over-seriously. But the day is not lost. There is hope. I knew it when I found a reader writing this:

> *We who love books,*
> *Have part in the creation,*
> *Of each new book;*
> *For, as imagination*
> *Inspired one man to write,*
> So it inspires
> Another man to read!

A ticket from the Epworth Press set my feet toward the *Sunday Times* National Book Fair. For a fortnight each year, I discovered, publishers, booksellers and book-lovers of Britain gravitated towards London. Books, posters, and ancillary trades' exhibits were spread over several floors of a great hall. And three times daily, distinguished authors, poets, publishers and dramatists came to lecture. From the moment Winston Churchill gave his blessing at the opening ceremony, till Ian Hay finished on *Atlantic Humours*, a fortnight later, it was a grand experience.

To my surprise the Epworth Press featured my book on their stall at the foot of the stairs. As suiting its title, *If I Open My Door*, its dust-jacket showed a green door, pleasantly ajar, leading into an enclosed garden, with a seat, and a glimpse of green things growing. It lent itself to this imaginative treatment. For the exhibition, an artist had been engaged to model it, and his attractive model stood centrally positioned on the stall—with crazy stone steps leading up to its open door, affording an entrancing glimpse within, a tiny concealed light suggesting sunshine.

Yet for all my pride in it, I was happier when I discovered that there was also a lift to the other floors, and I need not pass that very personal stall too often.

Without counting the Book Fair, the bookshops, publishers, and secondhand stalls in Charing Cross Road—though who would be so foolish—one can wander in and around London for ever in a book-lover's paradise. There are the fascinating manuscripts in the museums and the old houses. I shall never forget the day Rene and I spent at Dickens's house. It was good to recall there, among the things that were his, the shyness and joy that overcame him when his first work was published, and he had to turn into Westminster Hall for half an hour.

Another day we sought out Dr. Johnson's house, and for our midday meal, Ye Olde Cheshire Cheese—the oldest Chop House in London—where that wordy old genius used to meet with his cronies.

Yet another day we set off to find Carlyle's house. Chelsea is a part particularly rich in literary links. All the leading folk in Carlyle's day seemed to have repaired thither—many to his own fireside in Cheyne Row. Leigh Hunt lived in the white house just round the corner. Dickens was a guest. Tennyson visited to smoke a pipe. Mazzini, Ruskin, John Stuart Mill, Harriet Martineau, Emerson, Dean Stanley, Kingsley, Huxley, Lecky, all crossed the threshold.

We found it a fascinating house, apart from these links, restored as nearly as possible to its state when Thomas and his wife lived in it, quarrelled in it, were reconciled in it, and found through all the vicissitudes of life that love did not desert them.

There were many personal things in that house to see, between its 'sunk story' which served as kitchen, and its tiny sound-proof room at the top, where Carlyle sought refuge from the cursed crowing of cocks in the neighbourhood. It was thrilling to see his ink-well, his manuscripts, and his little desk that he took about with him.

A goodly number of visitors from across the Atlantic, we were told, come to Carlyle's house. I can only hope that some of them manage better than those who came whilst we were there. 'I have a party outside,' said the guide, addressing the caretaker within our hearing. 'But we've only got eleven minutes—what can you show us in eleven minutes?' In some distress, the old caretaker answered him, 'Really, if you've so little time, I wonder whether you ought to bother to come into Mister Carlyle's house.' But they did come in—and stayed long enough to buy a few postcards to prove that they'd been. I like to select each day's high-spot when travelling, rather than try to keep a complete diary. It might be something ancient, something beautiful, or something unexpected—a page of the Doomsday Book, a ride down Fleet Street—the street of paper and ink—the view toward Whitehall from St. James's Park at dusk, the misty blue under the trees in Kensington, the little old study of John Wesley's house

'TOGETHERNESS'—AS THE SUN CLIMBS
(At the end of our garden)

where are many of his books. It is good to collect such memories. But that is not easy, for London's offering to the book-lover is so rich.

One find in a library did however bring me down to earth with a bump. I had been a number of days at work in that gathering place of great things, when it occurred to me to see what they had on New Zealand. Assembled there was an impressive array of books on other parts of the world. But when I did find the section, it offered me but eight shabby little books, standing at drunken angles, the wording above them: 'Australia and the Polar Regions.' *We hadn't even a label to ourselves!*

XXIII

CHRISTMAS was memorable. We hung up our stockings—and wakened early to carols under the window.

And mid-morning, leaving 'Peter' with the turkey, mince pies, and pudding, we set off for Church.

Just on twelve, when we streamed out with the crowded congregation, it was all but impossible to see across the street. The street-lamps were amber blurs; even indoors there was a nimbus around the lights. We reached home just as 'Postie', over-burdened, was turning from our door. Hearing voices, 'Peter' had hastily sorted our New Zealand mail, and it awaited us when we entered. Never before had we so much as received mail on Christmas Day, and here was a bulging home mail!

It was quite dark when we sat down to dinner by the flicker of a wood fire, and the light of two tall red candles. When the great brown pudding came in, attended by a sauce, and set on a blue platter, it looked like the dome of St. Paul's riding the sky. Mistletoe hung in our tiny hall—mistletoe as we had seen it only on Christmas cards.

As the day wore on, friends popped in, the B.B.C. provided Dickens's *Christmas Carol*, and the fellowship and fun were good to share.

How eagerly we clung to those last few days! Early in the New Year, we knew we must once more concentrate on passports, bags, and all the bustling et ceteras of travel. So real was the present that it was nearly impossible for us to cast our minds back to the good old days, when 'travel' and 'travail' were interchangeable. In an old English guide-book, I came upon a solemn advertisement addressed to travellers like ourselves: 'How often is a night's rest disturbed by insect worries! If travellers will take some of XXX's celebrated Insect Powder, they can be freed from these annoyances. It kills Bugs, Fleas and Black Beetles.'

We had had no reason to be deterred by such things. Neither Rene nor I had ever met a black beetle farther afield than our own wood-shed.

But travel, for all that, can still be a strenuous undertaking. One's mind is on the stretch from morning till night; one's belongings must be sorted, packed and repacked a thousand times; one's person must be transported from 'bus to boat, and from 'plane to train; and I defy anyone to name anything so exhausting as being tramped around places of historic interest.

Ah, but the delights outweigh all the pains; the benefits outweigh all the botherations! To live and move outside one's own country, to see things ancient and lovely that have become part of the pageant of humanity, to find out how others of the world-family live, is an experience most rewarding.

As far back as 1785 a spirited member of my own sex was splendidly persuaded on this point. She sallied forth, brave soul, when 'travel' and 'travaille' were interchangeable in the realest sense of the word, before there were Cook's Agencies, popular travel books, or Travel Clubs. 'But nobody,' declared she with spirit, 'ought to be too old to improve. I should be sorry if I was. And I flatter myself,' she added, 'that I have already improved considerably by my travels. First, I can swallow gruel soup, egg soup, and all manner of soups, without making faces, much.' (I love that word 'much'!) 'Secondly,' added this seasoned traveller, 'I can pretty well live without tea; they give it, however, at Geneva. Thirdly, I am less and less shocked.'

Travel, of course, is only one-tenth geography, and nine-tenths a matter of the traveller. We have all met the lady who only remembered Rome as the place where Emmy matched her beads; we have all met the hopeless creature who has been all round the world, and has nothing to tell of it beyond the awful fogs in London and the beastly food in Belgium. It was for such that A. A. Milne added a word to a booklet put out by the Council for Education in World Citizenship—for those who leave home without the least hope of seeing anything so interesting anywhere else, hugging to their hearts the idea that their own country is the best country, and their country's way of doing things the best way of doing things. A. A. M. encourages humility and tolerance. He laughs at the traveller who proudly boasts that he, or someone in his party, can 'pronounce foreign names like a native', and reminds such of the story of the Red Indians who imitated the cry of the coyotes, 'and did it much better than the coyotes, *who are not really very good at it!*' His twinkle about traffic he leaves to each of his travellers to interpret as widely as possible in terms of tolerance. 'On the Continent,' says he, 'you will observe that the traffic takes the right-hand side of the road; not because that is the sort of silly thing that foreigners would do, but because they think that taking the left side of the road is the sort of silly thing that only the English would do.'

There is a good deal of truth for the traveller in the old saying: 'When you are in Rome, you must do as Rome does.' To long for 'Colonial goose' in Austria, for instance, is just to miss one of the delights of such travel. That coffee rather than tea is more generally served in Paris, is at first, surprise enough in itself. Rene and I will not soon forget the morning when—the master of the *pension* having persuaded us to try his 'British tea'—we allowed him to prepare us tea instead of the usual coffee and rolls. We should have known better. A knock on our bedroom door, four stories up, and in came the tray, with a pot of boiling-water—at least we suppose it was boiling when it started from the kitchen. But he hadn't put the tea in—it hung from the knob of the pot in a little muslin bag!

Language, of course, is another test for the traveller. In most places it is possible, with a little trouble, to find someone with a few words of English. Where that is out of the question, one is free to explore other ways of managing. When we were in Italy, we had only about five Italian words—and worked them till they were all out at the elbows. We did however manage to find out where to go, and what to eat, and what it would cost to eat. In France, I remembered that Rene had two impressive books on her shelves at home—prizes for French at Grammar School. But, alas, the people of France did not speak Grammar-School French! When we got to Germany I got a German-English dictionary. The very first night I took it to table with me. I like to know what I'm eating if at all possible. The soup on the menu that night ran itself into a word nineteen letters long. With the aid of my dictionary, I began to break it up into syllables—the word, of course, not the soup—and it came out to be 'the nourishment of the chicken, with semolina individuals'. And when it came, it was exactly that—chicken soup with bits of semolina floating about in it!

Our greatest adventure was at a camp in southern England. I have told of that in an earlier book. There were ninety of us, from eleven different countries. The boot was now on the other foot, when one of the Dutch girls came one morning with a difficulty as great as any we had encountered in her country. Behind the college where we were camped rose the Downs with their lovely curves. We walked over them, but they were a puzzle to our Dutch girls—and typical of a great deal that was puzzling. 'Your language,' said one, 'I never will learn it.' 'What is the matter with it?' I asked with a twinkle. 'It is so difficult,' said she. 'You say, for instance: "We will go over the Downs"—and you mean "we will go *over the ups*".'

When to the hazards of luggage and language, the challenge of a totally new way of life is added, things are likely to be even more interesting.

One of our campers was a delightful German girl, a refugee, a Doctor of Laws, speaking several languages, though her English was a little 'rusty'. At the end of Camp, she was guest in an English home.

A few days passed and we received a most amusing letter. 'All the time since I have left Camp,' she wrote, 'I am thinking of you, especially since I entered this marvellous castle. It is not a real castle, it is a fine old English country house, built in the best spot I ever have seen; but even it is a castle, for such things I have seen here and which happen here I never saw before.

'After one hour drive we arrived. One man servant opened the door of the car, another took my luggage. I had no time to see what kind of people they were, and what would happen with my precious violin, when another servant took my coat. After being introduced to the whole family of my friend (a helper at the first Camp I have been) I had a look into the lovely garden. We arrived very late, so it was just supper-time. My friend showed me my room. (I think it is the best room in the house because of its lovely view.) You will understand my being afraid when I noticed that a girl servant had taken all my things out of my luggage, and put them into twenty different draws and boxes. My only thought was: "God in heaven, what must she have thought of all my crumpled camping things." And I was extremely ashamed. My

194

long blue frock was spread over the bed, showing that I had to change for supper.

'Coming downstairs I found whole the family in beautiful evening dresses, and I tried to make a most happy face. The dining-room was lighted with candles. I counted four different man servants with extremely solemn faces. Once I thought, if I would say quite loudly, "*Bloody!*"—I learned this expression when I went with the Campers to the theatre—whether they would move their faces; but I decided not to try.

'The food was extremely good, and you will be sure I had not to ask for another time. There were a great many knives and forks which gave a good impression that it would not be necessary to ask for a second time. Do you wonder whether I felt quite happy? Half yes, half no. It is extremely strenuous to have such a good behaviour that you can join a party like this, even if it is "only the family quite alone".

'I slept well, till the maid knocked at my door, and came in with tea and butter and bread. A quarter to nine, we all were gathered in the big hall for morning prayers, taken by the father of my friend. There I saw the whole staff. I tried to count (just when we had not to pray), and I counted about eight girl servants, all in the same kind of frock, and four man servants, and three boy servants. I was deeply impressed by seeing these quantities.

'So I hope,' she finished, 'you will be not only a little bit jealous of my time here, but will feel pity also that it has been so difficult for me to have a good behaviour.'

Well! Well! Well!

XXIV

Our ship left on my birthday—the first I had ever had all to myself. It makes a neat little puzzle for children. A twin? And your twin sister still alive, and you had a birthday all to yourself? How was that? The answer is easy enough, once you know it. My twin sister was in New Zealand, of course, so the birthday had reached her first—and when she had enjoyed it and gone to bed, it came to me on the other side of the world.

Greatly enriched—though with empty purses—we waved our 'good-byes'.

Fourteen days and nights later we wakened to the swift knowledge that our ship was quiet, not plunging nor rolling, not pitching and groaning. We had come into Kingston. About our port-holes were wheeling gulls with querulous cries, behind us one of the most trying storms the ship had ever struggled through. She might, the captain was careful to say, have known a greater storm for a lesser time, but no storm of such battling madness for a longer time. The strain on the engines had been enormous. We had lost two days' sailing time. One particularly bad night—our second Sunday out—we had received S.O.S. calls from two boats in distress: from a Danish ship that had lost its top deck and its first mate overboard, and a Greek ship that had lost all its lifeboats. Happily, help had been available for those unfortunates earlier than we could get to them.

Six of us were listed for our chosen table, but we met only once. Rene was one of the valiant ones. Most mornings she managed at least to report for breakfast, though several times that was about all. I was not so courageous, though not actually seasick. Mighty waves, growing ever more angry and uncontrolled, smashed at our port-holes. The timbers of our ship strained and whined, the cabin-floor took on an uneasy angle.

Just how high were those waves? It is difficult to say. Distance—both perpendicular and horizontal—is deceptive at sea. My feeling about the Atlantic, I confess, was pretty much that of Robert Lynd: 'I do not whole-heartedly enjoy storms at sea, but I enjoy having been through storms at sea.' When we could struggle up on deck—and Rene and I were among the first to do so—the seas were still mountainous, and as we hung on to each other, and any immovable object handy, hugging our rugs about us, the gale snatched away our words.

Very different had been those long 'blue days at sea' of the Mediterranean voyage. We had enjoyed them fully, but in a calm, dreamy moment, Rene had expressed the wish that she might, just once, experience a storm at sea. The powers, it seemed, had taken her too seriously.

Jamaica was a joyous relief—the quiet, green beauty of it. Early in the morning, we wandered through the markets, and loaded ourselves up with baskets of fruit. The original inhabitants, the Arawak Indians—exterminated by the Spanish—called the island Xaymaca, meaning literally: 'The Land of Wood and Water.' The island we found richly blessed with these good gifts of earth and sky. Bananas growing in the hills and valleys gave an effect of a verdant mantle.

We rode through the sugar-cane fields and up into the hills. Some of the roads there, winding in and out, reminded us of our own bush roads, affording distant blue glimpses.

SC—G*

I chose to work part of every day from Jamaica on. I had undertaken to do some writing, and thoroughly enjoyed getting down to it.

For relaxation and a little fun mid-morning and mid-afternoon, I played deck-croquet for the first time in my life. And all unwittingly found myself the champion of the tourist-class. I counted it something of a lark to go up to the first-class deck to play off games with some very seriously croquet-minded matrons.

But it would have been a pity to have attempted anything in the way of work or play the day we passed through the Panama Canal.

It was all so different from what we had expected—from the narrow, straight-forward Suez Canal—the locks by which our ship was raised, and lowered, and the scenes along its fifty miles of length. On one of the slimy, sloping mudbanks, I saw my first crocodile dozing in the sun. It was not difficult at the day's end, to appreciate the epoch-making conquest of the Stegomyia and Anopheles mosquito, that all but wrecked the scheme.

We spent a hot, colourful day at Panama, the cathedral and university city at the southern end of the canal.

Pitcairn was our next—and our last call before home—though it was impossible to go ashore. It was pitch black when we approached the island, infamous for its part in the Mutiny of the *Bounty*. Nowhere, we knew, was a more thrilling story in the annals of the sea than how the last remaining mutineer, John Adams, found himself shut up in the little island, with a number of native women, a handful of children, and his own bitter memories.

Nor could we forget the dramatic way in which new life had come to the island—the secret of that new life, a

Bible, which John Adams found in a sailor's trunk. Transformed, himself, Adams had set about teaching the children, and lived to see the complete transformation of the little island, so torn by feuds, and drenched with blood.

Of his people, one visiting captain wrote: 'I think them a very humane and hospitable people; and whatever may have been the errors and crimes of Adams, the mutineer, in times back, he is at present a worthy man, and may be useful to navigators who traverse this immense ocean.' Pitcairn had become a hundred per cent Christian; nowhere on earth was life more safe.

As we drew near in the dense darkness, it would have been easy to have doubted its existence. Then as we peered over the ship's side we saw a tiny point of light—but whether near or far, it was difficult to tell. Then it disappeared altogether. We waited. Somebody suggested that it was a lantern.

Soon we were able to pick out the line of a boat coming toward us. Next moment we saw it was fully manned, but there was a heavy swell running.

We saw the men ship their oars, in an attempt to get in close, and clutch at a rope thrown them. But it was of no use. Their boat, tossed like an empty nut, was instantly carried astern. But quickly manœuvring their oars, they made another attempt. Again they were washed astern. A third attempt was more successful.

Once they had made fast the rope, we flung them a rope ladder. It hung giddily in space, like a toy thing, against the steep ship's side. Then someone in the bobbing boat put a foot on it, and heavily laden with fruit, started to climb, flung by the elements first inside and then outside the turning ladder. It was a too giddy sight for those of us who watched, and we stepped back, only to return with our cheers when the first islander came aboard—a woman! Others heavily laden followed her—also bare-footed; then came the children.

For an hour they stayed aboard, descendants of the *Bounty*, slow-moving, English-speaking people, trading their fruits and carvings for cash or old clothes.

We had been round the world. It was strange to see our own wharf, streets, and city from the view-point of new-comers, but as we drove homewards, through the be-gardened suburbs, it seemed a pleasantly exciting thing to be home.

XXV

Perhaps it is always painful to come to the cross-roads of choice. Between the end of this adventure in travel, and the beginning of a new one, there was a period when the choice I had to make reduced my weight and my sleep.

But looking back now, I can only be glad that I severed my connexion with the Mission. 'Buttons,' who had done my work whilst I was away, continued for a time. Then she sent in her resignation.

The Methodist Church was not yet ready to receive a woman into the full ordained ministry. So I plunged in to a branch of her service that had long held my heart.

Never had we been allowed to forget Wesley's great word: 'See that every home is supplied with books.' For years a book-room had served from the top-floor of a building on the main street of our largest city, but all New Zealand isn't streets. For some time we had had a 'book-room on the road' as well, but that service had lapsed. So the Department under which I had served in the country was ready for me to tackle the task.

Soon all my thoughts were on the new venture. I suppose I walked on solid earth those first days, but it hardly seemed that I did, the possibilities of the new job were so much after my heart. A new Bedford van, and a ten-foot trailer-caravan painted a soft grey—and I refused lettering on either—made up a fine unit. My territory extended over the whole country, my method of work something I had to puzzle out for myself. And a wonderfully rewarding adventure it was until four-and-a-half years later war brought me off the road.

By then I had travelled the length and breadth of the country; had worshipped and led worship in graceful-spired churches; shared the enthusiasms of my heart and mind with city audiences, and with little groups in remote places, with lads in 'borstals', nurses in common-rooms, workmen with a week's whiskers on, youngsters in schools and colleges, thinking the 'long, long thoughts of youth'. I had shared the intimate hospitality of many hearts, and an enthusiasm for life with people differing as widely in externals as farmers, and librarians, doctors, and bullock-drivers. I had done business with people doing every conceivable job, from nuns in a convent, to a sexton about his task in the graveyard. I had come to know well the countenance of every season, and had made friends with winds and weather.

In winter that was no easy task. But it's a poor heart that cannot extract some joy from conditions of misery. In summer, when the sun blessed every living creature, and country roads were a leafy way, friends would have come with me, but nobody volunteered to come in the winter when coats and shoes were wet all day.

I loved my little caravan, 'my grey house'. From centre to centre I moved it, and used the van to make my way round the countryside, so that on the dustiest or wettest day, I always had a clean place to call 'home'. It was very satisfying, when 'snugged up' inside, to be so close to the weather, and yet out of it. Sometimes in a parking-place, an old cow would come up and rub herself on my house, or on a perishingly cold morning, sheep, as much in need of warmth and comfort as myself, would snuggle in under it. Every fresh parking-place brought its adventures and its new set of noises and smells.

I like to look back now to my nights in the country, especially long starry nights and still, when I drove home late after a meeting, twenty or thirty wiggly miles—virtue gone out of me, and the rest of the day my own. But I hated always those nights when I had to hurry back to do book-keeping and re-ordering—nights that came all too often. If ever I lift up my eyes 'in hell, being in torment', I shall be doing long-tot sums and checking up cash-books.

It was a very strenuous life. Apart from the continual driving—the van, and caravan twenty-four feet in length —there were the planning and packing, the re-ordering, the continual meeting of new people, and the meetings. (In one part of the country, thanks to the 'unimaginative genius' of a committee, I did a hundred and thirteen meetings in forty days, added to hundreds of miles of travel. That, however, was an issue on which my Superintendent took a very strong view.)

After I had been travelling almost three years on the road I wrote a book. I called it: *A Thousand Sunrises*. But there was more than another year of sunrises after that, and some of the most rewarding.

I dedicated my book to Rene—as to 'a certain very delightful person,' adding,

> *Each day, dear love, my road leads far*
> *From where you, home-contented are;*
> *My mood is kin to that unrest*
> *Which sends the wild bird from its nest.*
>
> *But though I have a roaming heart,*
> *God gave me too, a homing heart.*

It is not easy really to know one's own country; there are first of all the difficulties of geography and time. Commercial travellers may be reckoned the most fortunate, but even they cover only a limited area, and meet people chiefly in hotel commercial rooms and places of business.

Overseas folk 'do' a set itinerary, and content themselves with tourist attractions; ordinary working folk get a holiday but once a year, and even with an occasional weekend, it takes a long time to get very far. I was fortunate—trebly fortunate—in covering the whole country, in meeting people in their own settings where most show up best, and in giving my whole time to it.

Throughout, I worked in close co-operation with the ministers of the church. This saved hours of time, and pointless travelling. It saved me also the indignity of door-to-door salesmanship. In each new place I met as many people as possible at a meeting or series of meetings. Then I sought out, in company with the minister, any who might be prevented from attendance, by reason of distance, sickness, or young families. And, of course, I sought out established book-lovers.

Nowhere, surely, can there be so many winding roads to the mile, so many climbs and corners; nowhere can there be so many kinds of gate-catches. But I chanced upon many 'adventures of mind and spirit' by way of them. I shall never forget those years.

One of the simplest services I remember I shared in a little country place.

The young parents entered with the babe, and the service of baptism began.

It was a beautiful service. And some words walked up and down in my mind: 'God gives us love—and something to love He lends us.' In that simple service, that loan seemed especially dear. For it was the practice of the minister to give to those who stood on holy ground, a printed reminder of the relationship. And I fancied, as the service went on, that I could hear those young parents poring over it on their return home—each reading it to the other:

> At first, we held him to be all our own,
> Until, across the font, in Holy Sacrament,
> We saw him as God's loan;
> No casual gift, but intimately lent
> Unto our human care.
> And then besprinkled in the Triune Name
> Over the passing names he was to bear,
> We took our vows to share his laud and blame—
> With his first Father, in the mystic tie
> Which binds the earthly to the Eternal family.

Much I knew would be missed from our life, but for the loan of childhood—little hands to clutch our stronger hands, little moods to try us sorely, little minds to pose questions beyond our poor answering—serving to lead us out beyond our little wisdom and strength to the wisdom and strength of the great Father.

But one little Child God would not lend. And of all that I thought upon in that quiet place, that was most wonderful —God had given us His Son, the Christ-child. Chaste words from Alice Meynell came to my mind to clothe the wonder, as I thought upon it:

> Given, not lent,
> And not withdrawn—once sent,
> This infant of mankind, this One
> Is still the little welcome Son. . . .
> New every year,
> New born, and newly dear,
> He comes with tidings and a song,
> The ages long, the ages long.

There is no glory like it. It is the truth that holds the world together. God has given His Son: no calculation mars the Divine bestowal. He comes to us as the Supreme Gift, outright, unutterable and for ever.

XXVI

Now when I look back, those years on the road help me to maintain a sense of proportion between timeless things like the sun on the hills, and transitory things like trade in town; for when the pattern is changed, it is not the hills that pass.

The first thing I was required to do on returning to sleep in a house, was to prepare a slit trench at the end of the garden, though there was doubt whether we would get Rene's aged mother down into it. The Japanese drew uncomfortably near; on land, sea and in the air, it seemed, they were making alarming progress, though it was difficult to get any clear idea of what was happening. The air-warden called, we prepared our first-aid kit, and checked our stocks of food. Those of us who knew that any service we might render would have to be on the home-front, rushed off to St. John's headquarters for 'brushing-up' lectures, and to local sports-fields, where the fire-brigade instructed us in the art of sand-bags, long-handled shovels, and incendiaries.

And months passed—*and the blow did not fall!*

Stories of bombing reached us and grim pictures of destruction, and of endless streams of refugees. Every home with a boy or girl serving in the forces—and there were few that were not in some way involved—lived from day to day, from hour to hour. Europe, and now Asia, were torn with the harsh sound of armed men, and the misery and suffering attendant on the machines of death. And there was no escaping the inevitable wireless-set—in every anxious home and work-shop—plugging away at its barrage of propaganda, dulling sensitive spirits, and blotting out the sweet outlines of truth. And months became years,

> *And lies bore lies,*
> *And lust bore lust,*
> *And the world was heavy with flowerless rods,*
> *And pride outran*
> *The strength of men*
> *Who set themselves in the place of gods.*

From the Continent came stirring words—from Albert Einstein, the famous scientist, a German Jew: 'Being a lover of freedom, when the Nazi revolution came to Germany,' said he, 'I looked to the universities to defend freedom, knowing that they had always boasted of their devotion to the cause of truth: but no, the universities immediately were silenced. Then I looked to the great editors of the newspapers whose flaming editorials in days gone by had proclaimed their love of freedom; but they, like the universities, were silenced in a few weeks. Only the Church stood squarely across the path of Hitler's campaign for suppressing truth. I never,' added the professor, 'had any special interest in the Church, but now I feel for it a great affection and admiration because the Church alone has had the courage and the persistence to stand for intellectual truth and moral freedom. I am forced thus to confess that what I once despised, I now praise unreservedly.'

Despite all the evil and waste of war, there were moments when it was a proud thing to be counted Christian, if it meant that one might stand along with Bishop Bergraav of Norway, Pastor Niemöller of Germany, Kaj Munk of Denmark, Kagawa of Japan.

And there were others, known more closely and loved more dearly because we had shared Christian fellowship.

H—— wrote from Czechoslovakia: 'Dear Friends— Thank you for your letter. I have been very happy reading that.' Then came this poignant little touch: 'How beautiful land must be your Fatherland, and how happy, because it is pretty far away from middle Europe. We are all sad and desperate, but all the suffering, blood and tears sees the most righteous God! He is going with us up on to the Golgotha!'

F. T.—— wrote from Holland: 'If I could tell you something of what people here have gone through, I would scarcely know where to begin.

'To give you an idea of the scale of the terror, and against whom it was directed, I need only tell you that in this part, of our six clergymen of the protestant Churches, five were sent to concentration camp. One of them, a man of sixty, was first marched through the town, down every back street, with two soldiers beside him and one with loaded revolver behind.

'Well, after that it never stopped; the Germans claimed our copper, our tin, our church bells, and every resistance they tried to quench by prison and concentration camp. The result was underground resistance on a large scale, and, as far as the schools and Churches were concerned, open resistance.

'Now I am writing this, I can hardly believe that we have really lived through all these things; that really the German machine-guns were at every corner of the streets here, and the men were driven from their houses like cattle in the pouring rain; that my brothers had to dive into their hiding-places at every alarm. That in one little village we know one hundred and two houses were burnt down, and over six hundred people driven to Germany, of whom only thirty returned, and they all invalids; that the staff of our school, together with the Board, secretly had to meet in order to discuss how to resist Nazi influence in the school. I still can see them huddled together in the dark attic of the school.'

From many other parts came stories of glorious courage. Even military officials and non-missionary-minded traders, had to admit that but for the loyalty and courage of the mission natives of the Solomons, Papua and New Guinea, there would have been no power to stop the Japanese invaders as they made their way south to Australasia. And that was a point in favour of missions that came home to many with new power all over the world. Our missionaries had served, and served so well—replacing the law and savagery of the jungle with a new spirit— that when the testing-time came, the natives had enough to be grateful for, to stand by with magnificent courage and loyalty. They led ambushed men to safety by little-known tracks, they rescued men shot down, they nursed and tended the sick, and they cared for the women and children with such a tenderness that a new content was given to the word.

And at great sacrifice prideful purposes of the invaders were defeated.

War brought in its train fear, bodily anguish, hunger, and a thousand evils, but there were moments when there were revealed things of lasting worth. One moved often from the noisy, ugly front of war, to within the quiet ramparts of the soul.

Something had gone from Rene and myself with the death of 'Buttons'—at the same time something had been added. For her life had been a swift adventure.

During those days, I set myself to write a book about those who served the things of the spirit in the Pacific. I called it, in contradiction to the old slogan: *'Safety Last.'* Much that I was able to gather had never been committed to writing before. In many cases, I took down the facts first-hand, and those who kindly allowed me to re-tell their stories were able to check my manuscript.

Letters were being lost at sea through enemy action, so every effort to check facts at a distance had to be done in duplicate and triplicate. And the task became a long and difficult one.

I wanted my stories to observe no order of selection, save that of spirit—so that time, place, colour and deno-mination could be shown to matter less and less. It was fitting that an American Christian should rub shoulders with a wearer of the British Empire Medal, and an islander of the battle-scarred Solomons, with a German priest of the jungle.

It was a satisfaction that the book received so real a welcome. 'No one,' said one reviewer, 'can be sure where the focus of the next ten years will lie, but it is certain that the Far East, and particularly the Pacific Ocean, will be vastly important.'

Safety Last was my seventh book. Following on three of letters, I had written two books of journeys—one cover-ing our walking in the south of England, and one my years of caravanning. Like Pliny, I confess: 'I love to renew a pleasure by relating it.'

The other was a slender volume of devotions, of a kind different from anything I had come upon—twenty-one meditations, each with a beautiful photographic study. I called it, *While the Candle Burns.* I made it first for my own soul's help during those war days, which were also for me days of further illness and uncertainty. The truth and beauty of George Meredith's words were much with me: 'The light of every soul burns upward; but most of them are candles in the wind.'

Despite war and hate and ugliness, my heart said the world was still God's world. It was still richly blessed with beautiful things—literature, song, laughter, loyalty, courage and all the inner qualities of the human spirit. And I tried to gather together some of those things. I sought them in many countries—a picture of a cross at sundown, from Austria, an English nurse bending at her duty in a London that had been under the blitz, a glimpse of the eternal hills from the altar of a little chapel in our own mountains; and Holland gave me a picture richly suggestive of the realities 'hidden from our eyes, beyond the hills of Time'.

Some of the most moving letters that reached me during those days concerned that little book. It was being used by people in places of ugliness where war had led them, in times of strange testing and hurt, in times when the body as well as the spirit was bowed with exceeding weariness. One wrote from Holland that she had translated it for her class. Another wrote from England—the only remaining member of her family after the blitz. She had not been to the church for eleven years, but life had become so overwhelming that she had gone alone to the cathedral to pray. On her way back, walking slowly, she had espied a book in a shop window—a slender book: *While the Candle Burns*. Next day she wrote to me: 'I've never written to an author before; but before the night was at an end, I'd found my way back to God. I felt I had to write and tell you.' From Glasgow, a padre wrote: 'My finding of that little book of devotions, it is not too much to say, marked a spiritual experience in my life.'

Where does a miracle like that end? But then everything about writing is a miracle. A writer can make little of this wide kingdom of literature without taking the shoes from off his feet. He must give up pondering how it can be that twenty-six letters, set down in endlessly different combinations can convey to strangers across the world—something which is eternal. He only knows that it is so.

I shall not forget a little letter that the post brought me, from a German-Jewish refugee friend. She had come to our land just as hostilities had broken out. When the situation was particularly grim, she wrote to me: 'In the world is so much evil, and so much suffering, that sometimes it is difficult to go on. But,' she added, '*I won't get lost* —lost means if I should become bitter, and lose my good spirit.' It was this gallant soul who wrote: 'I like the spirit which comes to me out of your book. I feel with you the joy in the subtle and in the overwhelming beauties of nature. I like your attitude to people, because it is full of understanding, kindness and responsibility. I like your twinkling humour, and I respect your understanding for the deep needs of life. Books like yours are so needed, I think. You are giving people a sense of responsibility toward one another, and a sense of reverence toward life and nature—the universe. That is so important, because many people do not care to penetrate below the surface of anything. There is too little desire to understand—to respect—to care. But we all must do it. All this I found in your book. . . .'

I can think of no more lasting reward than that people should find in a book of mine what she says she found there. Authorship as I know it, is an enlargement of life, an enrichment, a responsibility. How long does it take to write a book? It takes the whole of life; it takes everything that has made one the kind of person one is; it takes all that one has of natural gifts and graces, and a great deal more—a disciplined mind, and honest hard work. That publishers reward one is not to be overlooked, but it is not the main thing. The main thing—for author and readers alike—is that books enrich our awareness of living.

XXVII

I HOPED there might be only a brief interval before peace came, and I could return to the caravan—but the years dragged on. And I was still doing what I could to help in the Bookroom, when it was moved down to better premises on the street level.

It was good, I knew, that a writer should be in close touch with life—and with the stream of new books and the book-loving clients. None of those hours were wasted, though when I could, I grasped the opportunity to be freed from the need to work late into the night, to correct type-sheets on safety-zones, and galley-proofs on tram stops. Time had always been the most precious thing in my writing life. But I knew that a writer could not create in a void. So I arranged to give three afternoons a week to the Bookroom, and to divide the remainder of my time between writing, and other ploys. I was already responsible for an article in the church paper—which I had served for ten years—and there were occasional contributions to be made to overseas papers, including the oldest magazine in the English language—founded by John Wesley in 1778. Photography for my books also took up a lot of time, together with making and showing colour movie films, broadcasting, and attendance on lectures in English Literature. And there was no week when my services as preacher and speaker were not sought by some group—guild, association of students, little country church, city churches, travel clubs and literary societies. I liked them, I admired them, I wished them every kind of good, but I simply could not go and speak to them all.

Had I done that, I should have had no time left for writing.

I learned much in that Bookshop. 'A good bookshop, after all,' says Harold Laski—and I liked to remind myself of it—'is one of the supreme temples of the human spirit.'

It is an odd thing, but one has little idea of the diverse needs of men and women until one opens a shop—'the whereabouts of the Bank', 'the handiest butchers', 'the little shop that sharpens scissors'. One day, whilst I was deep in talk with a traveller, an old lady popped her head round a display of books to ask, ''Ave yer got any 'air-nets?'

But it can't be only the corner position of our shop that made it so easy to pop into with a thousand human requests, for we had our share when we were still upstairs. In one day I remember somebody at the end of the 'phone asking, 'Is that the Epworth Bookroom? Would you mind putting your head out of the window and telling me the time by the Town Hall clock?' 'No, not at all.' A few minutes later, someone serving as secretary in a small guild, rang: 'Could you tell me please, how to spell "conversazione"?' 'Well, no,' I had to reply, 'I'm afraid I can't—but I have a dictionary. Just a minute.' My next interruption was made in person—by a very dashing young woman standing on the threshold. Tall of stature, she carried style with her, and a handsome red bag that exactly matched her nails and make-up. Rising, I approached her with: 'Can I help you?' 'Oh, I do hope you can,' she replied soulfully, 'I want to find out about the seven devils.' 'T-h-e s-e-v-e-n d-e-v-i-l-s?' I repeated, and my mind flashed back to all the mentally distraught folk I had had dealings with. And I turned hastily on my heel to attempt some kind of concentration by looking at the packed shelves.

'Oh, but I don't want it out of a book,' she added. 'I want it for a lecture to-night.'

And then it dawned upon me: 'Do you mean the seven devils in the Scriptures—where the house was swept, and they all came back again?'

'Yes, yes, that's it,' said my soulful lady. Relieved, I took a concordance that lay on a desk, sought out the word 'swept', found the passage in the Gospel, and read it. 'Now that's wonderful,' said she, 'that's wonderful. I am grateful to you. That's wonderful!' And whilst she was so overwhelming with her thanks I showed her out.

Just then the tea-bell rang in the far office, and with other members of staff I trailed through. With my first cup, I related the story of my interruptions, ending with, 'I hope the Kingdom of God is greatly served by all these bits and pieces.'

'I think,' said our accountant half-seriously, 'we ought to have a place in our pay-sheets for all this kind of thing—for time wasted.'

'Oh, I don't know,' I added, 'in any case it would be a little difficult to compute. Take that last one: what would that be worth—about one-and-ninepence?'

'One-and-ninepence!' butted in our office wit, '*one-and-ninepence? Seven devils at threepence each*—that ought to be cheap enough!'

The same part-time assistant found herself a little non-plussed one day when she came to lend me a hand. I allowed her to attend to one of our old customers who came every year to select the Sunday-school prizes; it was her proud boast that she had done it for twenty-three years—*a very doubtful boast*. I knew she was not one to trust the morals of her tiny school to the staff of the Bookroom. She had to glance through each book before she bought it, and it took time.

215

When I returned from the bank, and lunch, an hour and a quarter later, she was still at her task. But I could see that my assistant's enthusiasm was definitely wilting. I suggested she might take her lunch-hour.

When she returned, I was just getting the old lady into the lift.

'What a customer!' was my friend's first remark.

Cheering her, I added: 'But she's nothing like so bad as another one we have.'

'Oh, I thought she was awful.'

'Well, she may be, but she is nothing like so bad as the other old lady,' I added unwittingly—'she just comes in the morning and takes off her hat and gloves and stays!'

Happily, through the years, there remained genuine book-lovers, and boys and girls and students—devotees at 'the temple of the human spirit.'

Whilst still under the shadow of war, a little old body came in one evening. 'I know you are just closing,' said she, 'but I wanted to pop in for a moment. I've just come from the opposition bookshop; they sent me here. I've been lately in hospital—a new experience for me. I shared a room with a Mrs. Regan. She had lost one of her boys in a prisoner-of-war camp, and her other boy, whilst running for a 'bus in leave time, had met with an accident, and lost both his feet.

'I was very ill, too,' she added, 'but when I was somewhat better, and could take an interest in things again, I noticed Mrs. Regan reading a green book. Sometimes she read me bits out of it, and one day I said to her: "Mrs. Regan, let me have a lend of your green book." And she did, and for the rest of our convalescence it was either on her bed or on mine. Extending her hand, she added, 'I just learned that you are here, and I thought I'd pop in and tell you what you did for us. She was Catholic, of course, I am Presbyterian, and I have just learned that you are Methodist.'

Some came seeking advice, some for a talk, some for a new book. And, of course, the mail came often to that little shop. Sometimes it was full of parcels—books for the shelves—but often there were letters. One came from a Scottish Doctor—an authority on astronomical and historical subjects, sometime holder of a famous lectureship. He said: 'I first came on *The Winds Blow* when I was feeling depressed because of the war—to me a heartbreaking sorrow. And I must say that it helped me in a way which no other book at the time was capable of doing. Having re-read the book for the third or fourth time, I felt it would be wrong if I did not write you and tell you something of what was in my mind.'

One day there was a letter from a club-leader in one of the over-crowded places of the earth. She wrote: 'We began this club thirty-five years ago—with four girls— in what was virtually only a covered-in yard between a fried fish shop and a public house.' And she went on to speak of the inspiration that books had been to her, and sent me a personal word. That club—moved to better premises when the slum was cleared—has now a membership of three hundred.

Then there came a letter from the director of a Braille Library, seeking permission to put some of the books into braille for the blind. And a group of enthusiastic teachers wanted to put a book of children's stories into Welsh.

And I shall not forget one of many that reached me at the little shop bearing the wings of the Air Force and the motto. 'One day,' it began, 'passing through Leeds on my way home, I bought *The Winds Blow*. . . . Then came Mother's operation, with the surgeon's revelation that she had not more than a few months to live. Dad gave up his work to nurse her: I came home as often as possible. And all the time *The Winds Blow* was ever fresh. With her Bible, it became Mother's daily companion, and as a family, we sometimes volunteered to read a chapter aloud. The doctor was amazed at her faith and courage, her strong spirit and her unfailing heart. Month after month she lingered on. . . . Knowing that the end was near, I got special leave. Night after night in the quiet watches, I read extracts from *The Winds Blow*, always concluding with: *God keep a clean wind blowing through my heart night and day*. . . . Then after sitting alone at her bedside for sixteen consecutive nights, at the end of nine months—my father was exhausted, and I had to arrange for him to do the day duties only. Mother she passed away quietly.

'Finally, when Dad, my sister and I gathered round her for the last time, I with great difficulty read aloud that great little prayer:

'*God keep a clean wind blowing through my heart night and day*.

'Since, I've been overseas, and whilst there I vowed that I would write to you when I returned to say "thank you" for all the good things you have written and for the place you have in our home.'

XXVIII

I can never forget that as children we invented a game—
to beguile the interval between bedtime and the coming of
sleep. We were put to bed far too early; but what children
are not? It was called 'Jography'—though when we were
a little older it was called 'Geography'. It was the same.
Each letter of the alphabet was used to call up a place-
name. I might begin with A—A for America; and my
sister follow with A for Australia; then I might add A for
Anderson's Creek. But I forget—you do not know Anderson's Creek, a little trickle down the end of my grandfather's farm, where we used to catch cock-a-bullies in the
summer-time.

We might get down to C, and possibly to D the first
night; down perhaps as far as H the second night; but it
usually took a third or a fourth to get down to my favourite
letter—that great, big letter with his tongue out, Q. My
sister could never think of anything for Q—only the
Queen—and I wouldn't let her count. But by some
mysterious insight, I knew that Q was for Queensland.

Guess then my delight a year or two ago, when a letter
reached me from the Methodist Church in Queensland,
asking me to be one of its centenary-year speakers.

But before I could sit on my luggage, and tie on my
labels, three other letters came—one from New South
Wales, one from Victoria, one from South Australia. The
first said, 'We hear you are going to Queensland. You
can't, of course, go to Queensland, without coming
through Sydney; come and take some meetings for us.'
The next one said: 'Come to Melbourne. You know this
gracious city; you know some of its people, and love its

trees—it's no great distance from Sydney. We'll fly you.'
And then came a similar plea from Adelaide. 'We will be
right into the swing of our end-of-year activities—and we
have a broadcasting-station. Come and meet with us.'

So it came to pass that in four rich months of incessant
travel, I compassed in all eighty-eight major meetings,
and a considerable number of 'major eatings'. During the
same time I received, and answered, some nine-hundred-
and-sixty letters from perfect strangers. And day after day
there fell to my lot mayoral welcomes, speeches, and
banquets. It was not hard for me to understand what
Field-Marshal Montgomery said about Australia, that it
was the place where there were fewer people to the square
mile, and more speeches to the square meal than anywhere
else on God's earth!

But if I am also to measure life by its times of spiritual
elation, there can have been few more vivid than those
four months.

I flew the Tasman—those twelve hundred temperamental miles that divide our two countries. I was glad
about that; I once crossed it by sea—and I have a very
good memory. I was even more pleased when a friend
wrote, as I was leaving, that she had just crossed by sea,
and had had a very rough trip. Flung hard against the
boat-rail, she had 'got a split lip and a split rib and a split
scalp *in a split second*!'

That morning when I left the air-base, there was a
satin-like sheen of loveliness on the water; but we had
not been many hours out when we were whipped and
wet by a terrific storm, and there was not one of us—
seasoned travellers all—but was glad to see that place-
name 'Sydney' materialize.

I can speak but little of my stay in Sydney—save to
mention the hospitality of Leigh College, days up in the
Blue Mountains, the trip to Sublime Point, and our great

meetings. It was a rare experience to be treasured in the memory, like an opal of many colours.

As a lover of books, I was glad to be able to help with the founding of a library for the women students of Leigh College. It was suggested, after I had done one or two meetings, that we ought to take up a collection for a library. 'And,' said those responsible , 'we would like to call it the "Rita Snowden Library".'

'But wait a moment,' I found myself interjecting, 'I'm not dead yet. In any case, I haven't a chink of thought left for a matter like this when I'm going into a big meeting.'

But they had already thought about it, they assured me, and if I would give my consent, they would like to go ahead with it. No genuine book-lover anywhere could hold back from such a request!

That I was able to crowd so much into those nights and days, was due in no small measure to the organizing genius of my friend, A. G. M. . . . I tried to say as much at a public luncheon tendered me before I left. For the rest, 'One can never pay in gratitude; one can only pay in kind, somewhere else in life—unconsciously, perhaps.'

Too soon I had to take leave of my new friends. We stood talking together at the aerodrome—still trying to say some of the things, for which in our secret hearts we knew there were no words.

Then from somewhere a loud-speaker awoke, and forty-four of us streamed out on to the air-field towards an aluminium-sheathed monster. A young air-hostess received us, showed us into our seats, and gave us barley-sugar out of a little dish. 'Good children,' I fancied I heard her say. We were all good children.

Slowly the monster moved along the ground. *Zoom-zoom-zoom!* Suddenly the noise increased, till it sounded like a million bee-hives—and we were off!

Up over the spready city we soared, home to a million

and a quarter people, up over its red roofs and its colourful coastline, fringed with white surf. And I fell in love with Sydney all over again. Unbidden, Anthony Trollope's words came to my lips: 'I have seen nothing to equal it, nothing second to it. It is so inexpressibly lovely.'

But in a very short time I was down again—down on the landing-strip in Brisbane—meeting another little company of strangers waiting to become friends. I found one of the things that made air-travel so strenuous was that one had no sooner shaken off the responsibilities of one group, and relaxed, than it was time to powder one's nose, and come down to meet another group, and a fresh set of responsibilities.

But what a wonder was air-flight! One's sense of size, speed and time utterly revolutionized! Not until my first flight—though it was in a single-engined 'plane, a frail thing that the boys might have made in the back yard—did I fully know the beauty of stretching country-sides, clouds and skies!

In Australia I found the distances so great, that in many cases, air-flight was the only way to travel.

From Brisbane—that colourful capital of that great State seven times the size of Great Britain—I flew a thousand miles north; up over islands, palm-fringed and beautiful, set in cobalt blue seas, over great stretches of jungle, the trees like parsley-beds. Every now and again we came down to re-fuel, when an unexpectedly flat piece of ground appeared, with frail sheds and little ants running about. Each time, as we drew near, one of the little ants was seen to be wearing a white collar, and each time as I stepped on to *terra firma*—the size of all things greatly increased—he turned out to be the Methodist minister come to welcome me!

Once or twice I watched the dawn come; twice I flew

into a tropical sunset; once I came in over a lighted city at midnight.

Thousands of surface miles by car and train were other experiences.

I made a coloured film of that journey, that I might be able to share some of its beauty. I called it 'Sunlit Journey'. But much of lasting worth and significance could have no place in a film. Above all, it was a spiritual experience—an adventure of giving and receiving. Everywhere people gathered hopefully, some from long distances. In the cities crowded congregations in themselves were a challenge. Such demands were not easily met; there was required instantly and continually, what C. E. Montague called: 'A new kind of living, a self-forgetfulness, a getting above ourselves, as artists do when they are at the top of their form, and saints in their ecstasies, and lovers in their in-loveness.'

Before we separated, six thousand of us poured out in procession to a green spot on the centenary day, to stand under the sky, and to thank God for what a hundred years had wrought. On that green spot—just a hundred years earlier—had stood one man and one woman—Reverend William Moore and his wife—the Methodist staff in that great State. Their courage might easily have failed them—thank God it did not!

For that special service I was privileged to be one of the two speakers. So much there was in that day that one should never forget. I spoke on the words: 'Never forget!' 'Never forget this historic spot; never forget those who planted the Church here; above all, as Paul wrote to young Timothy, "*Never forget Jesus Christ risen from the dead*!" '

I had a link with the early days, in the companionship of W. H. Green, the Centenary treasurer—son of the foundation members of the Primitive Methodist Church. When Charles Green and his young wife and family reached Brisbane as settlers, the vast State was scarcely four years old. The Captain-General had only surmounted his initial difficulties. To the Under-Secretary for the Colonies, he had written: 'I started with just $7\frac{1}{2}$d. in the Treasury. A thief—supposing, I fancy, that I should have been furnished with some funds for the outfit, so to speak, of the new State—broke into the Treasury a few nights after my arrival, and carried off the $7\frac{1}{2}$d. mentioned. However, I borrowed some money from the banks until our revenue came in.'

Only the year before Charles and Eliza arrived, sugarcane had been grown in the State for the first time, 'by an enterprising man, who using a lever for crushing the cane, and a saucepan as boiler, made the first pound of Queensland sugar.'

Charles was number one local-preacher on the first plan—and local-preacher, class-leader and Sabbath-school superintendent he remained for fifty years.

But times were not easy, and the firm that employed him as a moulder failed, owing considerable back pay. The young couple were already carrying a burden too heavy for human shoulders, for in their home a little child lay dead, and they had not money enough to bury her. Mercifully, a good friend came to the rescue.

Striking proof of the character of the young couple lay in the fact that during all the hard times they knew, Charles kept a careful account of the collections they had not been able to give to the Church, and when times were better, made *them up to the last penny*!

After years, they moved to Mackay, in the north, and it was there during my Centenary itinerary, that I came across a plaque on the walls of Mackay Church. It had not been forgotten that for years Charles had saddled his horse on a Saturday, after a hard week's work in the foundry, and ridden the rough bush tracks to preach to the folk on Sunday; that for years he had been a stout supporter of Methodist Union, and fittingly, Chairman of the Primitive Methodist Connexion at the time of Union. The drink he had fought as fearlessly through all the years, and it was as a tribute to his fair fight, that when he died, and his funeral passed by, every hotel closed its doors.

It was a lot to travel hundreds of miles with the son of that pioneer couple. Two of his brothers had been local-preachers for forty years—and three of them Sunday-school superintendents for almost as long. The son with whom I travelled, had served also as Mayor of Towns-ville, Deputy Leader of the Opposition, Grand Master of the United Grand Lodge of Freemasons. The wife of the Methodist Field Secretary was a grand-daughter of the same pioneer family; and the wife of the Choir-conductor for the Centenary celebrations another. Mabel Brown, the first lady missionary to the Indians in that part where at last she gave up her life, was another. A young grand-son—before his death at twenty, when life was just open-ing before him—was co-founder of a remarkable boys' class from which had come four young ministers, and a number of fine lay-workers—three for Queensland, and one for the overseas mission field.

It was written into the Book, I knew, that 'God visits the iniquity of the fathers upon the children, unto the third and fourth generation', but in Queensland I saw as clearly written into life *that God visits the good deeds of good fathers and mothers unto the third and fourth generation.*

XXIX

I ENJOYED making *Sunlit Journey*. For a photographer, Australia has great beauty. In the far north I saw lakes and waterfalls, exotic flowers and blue skies. Twenty-seven people there asked me—as an opening sentence—if I had seen the Barron Falls, Lake Eacham, and the Cascades: twenty-seven people had asked me if I had seen water in abundance—the miracle of water in abundance! And I sensed at once the importance of water to Australia. Coming from a land rich in rivers and waterfalls, I was more eager to see a blue-tongued lizard, to learn how a coconut falls, and a crocodile looks in his native *habitat*. I was more eager to see great forests offering beautiful timbers and strange ferns; to see in cultivated parts, crops commonplace to those who grew them—arrowroot and cotton, coffee and ginger. And there were delicious fruits.

In one place, when it became known how I enjoyed a pineapple, a fresh one arrived for me every night. It was often eleven or twelve before my day's work was finished, and I could get to my pineapple over the bath—but I never let a little thing like that deter me. But I must confess that I was often two and three pineapples behind myself!

Fresh bananas were another joy. Again and again I recalled the school-boy's essay on the banana. 'The banana are a great and remarkable fruit. They are constructed in the same architectural style as sausage, the difference being the skin of the sausage are habitually consumed, while it is not advisable to eat wrapper of banana. The banana are held aloft while consuming:

sausage are left in reclining position. Sausage depend for creation on human beings or stuffing machine; banana are pristine product of mother earth. In case of sausage both conclusions are attached to other sausage; with the banana the opposite termination are entirely loose. Finally, banana are strictly of vegetable kingdom, while affiliation of sausage is often undecided.'

Among growing things in the great continent, nothing held for me greater surprise than the pest cactus, 'prickly pear'. Little was known of its origin, I found, but it seemed certain that a treasured specimen had been carried from Sydney to Scone in the early days; certainly Queenslanders had grown hedges of the 'pear' round their homesteads. However the fleshy green pest got its start, by the turn of the century it covered ten million acres—and worse was to follow—twenty years later it covered sixty million acres.

But I had difficulty in finding *one specimen to photograph*! Throughout that vast area, menaced by the invader, a miracle had occurred. An innocent-looking little creature, *Cacto-blastis cactorum*—multiplied many million times—had effected the miracle. I can appreciate the gratitude of the people, though I was intrigued to find in one place, where the smiling earth looked up to the skies, a memorial hall raised to the little conqueror. It was the first time I had come across a memorial to an insect!

Many other strange forms of life found their way into my film—orchids in great variety, frilly lizards, snakes and laughing-jackasses, kangaroos and wallabies.

'What exactly do you want to see?' asked my host at a cattle-station up in the hills. 'I want to see the normal things,' I replied, as always when asked that question. 'I want to see your homes, and your gardens.'

'Would you like us to bring down some cattle?' he asked, his eye on my movie camera.

'But isn't this a working day?' I queried.

'Yes, but we could bring you some down,' he added. 'Would a couple of hundred be enough?'

I replied as casually, that I thought I could manage with a couple of hundred.

'Where will you have them?' was his next question. And at his suggestion, I picked a place in a field, and began secretly to wonder what I would do with two hundred cattle. In half an hour, three mounted men and a girl who joined them, brought down my two hundred beasties, and ran them round me three or four times in the form of a figure eight—and I stood in their midst all 'brave and fearless like', my knees trembling.

'You have seen much of the fertile edge of the land,' said my organizer friend later, when we sat comparing notes, 'what a pity it is you can't see the middle.'

'But how does one see the middle?' I asked.

'Well, you could go up to Alice Springs from Adelaide by train,' said he, 'five days up across the desert. But of course, it would be hot. December is a hot month. If it should be that "Old Griff" were there—the Reverend Harry Griffiths, Director of our Inland Mission, who, with Mrs. Griffiths, has been there for twenty odd years—he could show you a lot in a fortnight. But if "Old Griff" were off perhaps, on one of his long patrols, you might just as well stay south and save your money.'

I wondered very much about that journey, but as the time drew near, it became possible to fly, instead of that long five day's train journey up across the desert. Furthermore 'Griff' came out of the Inland every few years for a great conference—and this was the year for him to come. Indeed, this was the month for him to come—and as I walked out of my last meeting in Adelaide, a slightly-built man came towards me, sun-bronzed, and with a merry twinkle, and a grip like a man of the Inland. And it was 'Griff' come to join me.

I had made some effort to prepare my mind for the totally different world I knew the Inland to be. I had read a few books, and seen a film, and talked with Charles Mountford, known internationally among scientists for his knowledge of those parts. But I had got a number of things quite wrong. I knew we were to fly up over the desert, but I thought of desert as endless grey sand—as I had seen in other parts of the world. But this desert was colourful—from the air, there were blues and mauves and pinks. And when we came down there were great rocks and gaps of a 'fiery cinnabar'. And there were endless dry river-beds and mighty mountains. The MacDonnel Range alone stretched three hundred miles.

There was sand, of course, in places—plenty of it. I need tell only of Mr. and Mrs. 'Inland'. Mr. Inland was employed by the Railway company. His job consisted in sweeping the sand off the railway-line, which didn't sound very exciting, because it always blew on again.

Once a month, the train put them off a tank of water, and a box of rations. And once a year, Mrs. Inland went up to Alice Springs to do her shopping. She came up whilst I was there, to my delight, so I was able to meet and talk with her.

A little before my visit, the Governor of South Australia, Sir Winston Duggan, and his Lady, had made that long journey by train to Alice Springs. And in their journeying, of course, they had come to the home of the Inlands. They had seen the water go off, and the rations go off; and Sir Winston had said to his Lady, 'I wonder who lives in this little house. Come along, we'll go in and see.'

Understandably, Mrs. Inland was a little embarrassed to have Vice-regal visitors on the doorstep. She didn't quite know what to do; and to put her at her ease, Sir

Winston had said, 'Aren't you going to make us a cup of tea?'

Mrs. Inland had thought of that. 'Yes,' said she, 'I was going to make you a cup of tea, but I don't know whether I can. We haven't got any cups, we've only got mugs.'

'Oh, that's all right,' said Sir Winston, 'we'll have it out of mugs.'

But still Mrs. Inland seemed ill at ease. Then out it came, her trouble, all at once. 'I'm afraid that if I make you a cup of tea, it won't be a very good one, because last week the goat died, and we haven't any milk.'

'Oh, that's all right,' said Sir Winston, 'we'll have it without.' And they did.

Then they rejoined their train, and at the end of days, arrived in Alice Springs. At once, Sir Winston said to his aide, 'Now, before we become involved in business here, do this thing for me: go round the town, and buy me a couple of goats. And put them on this train that we've come off, and send them down into the desert with my compliments, to Mrs. Inland.'

And he did. And the vice-regal goats went down into the desert!

That serves as a reminder now, of more than the fact that there was sand in the desert—it speaks also of the loneliness of some of the people who make their homes there. In many ways I found a cruel country, beyond the hazards of loneliness, distance, and heat.

Seventy odd years ago—for the reasons that we know—a little company of young men, Lutheran missionaries, went up from Adelaide. They were young, they were keen, they were fit. They took some three thousand sheep, thirty-three horses and seventeen head of cattle. But the hazards of the way were so great, the heat so excessive, the going so cruel, that they didn't get to their destination till seventeen months had gone by. And when they did get there a great part of their precious live-stock had perished. Furthermore, they discovered they had been sent to found a mission on the bank of the river Finke, *seven hundred miles* from the nearest railhead, so that when their homes were established and they needed flour, it cost them seventy pounds a ton for carriage alone. More disquieting was the fact that the people they'd come to serve just weren't there—for three months they never saw one of them—then a few came out and had a little peek at them.

But they stayed—for the reasons that we know—stayed for thirteen years, until their little graveyard had begun to fill, and their purses had begun to empty. And they'd got nothing to show for it, save that the Aranda language had been reduced to writing, and the long tedious task of translation had begun. And they said, 'It's too costly!'

Their decision was received down at head-quarters, and on their staff was a Reverend Carl Strehlow, and his wife. He said, 'But that is not the way to deal with the desert. You must never give up. That is not the way to win. Someone else must go!'

And those two journeyed up to that place of failure— and stayed, stayed till they had wrenched success from that failure. For twenty-six years they stayed, till the old Pastor himself needed a doctor, and the nearest doctor was four hundred miles away across the desert.

The only way to get to him was by horse and buggy. So the black boy harnessed up the horse, and made his master as comfortable as he could. And they set off, and drove on and on. And they almost did it—they got within fifty-six miles of their destination. Then the old pastor could go no farther. So the black boy propped him up with cushions as best he could, and put a bit of a bough shade over his head. Then he took the horse from the shafts, and rode on to find a woman. He found her at the Horse Shoe Bend, and she rode out, and together they brought the old pastor in. And his grave to-day is at the Horse Shoe Bend.

I met the son of the old pastor, who as a lad had known no playmates but the little aboriginal children. He had spoken, of course, German, the language of his father and mother; he had spoken the language of the Aranda tribe; and to-day, Master of Arts with first-class honours, he is English language and literature lecturer in the Adelaide University—a very distinguished son of Australia. He had just come back from an extensive journey in that great country, when I met him, and spent an afternoon with him at the University, going over chants and legends he had collected. When published, they ought surely establish for all time the fact that Australia's black people have produced some of the most exquisite primitive verse yet discovered. They can no longer be counted a people so low in human intelligence that they have no sense of God—an old idea widely circulated—providing a sort of living link with the Stone Age.

I was guest at Hermannsburg—the scene of Pastor Strehlow's service. The Mission, I found, stood, as originally intended, on the bank of the river Finke—the longest river in Australia—a thousand miles long. The present pastor and his wife came as a young married couple, to carry on the work in the place of the old pastor. Said Mrs. Albrecht, in her charming German-English: 'When we heard that we were to serve a mission on the bank of the river Finke, a thousand miles long, I said to my husband: "A thousand miles long! It will be a very great river, and vessels will come up like the Elbe. And we shall have a swim, every morning we shall have a swim".'

And they came, the poor darlings, to their talks on the bank of the river Finke—a thousand miles long—and lived there for four years, and never saw *one teaspoonful of water in the river Finke! There just wasn't any!*

Whilst I was at Alice Springs, the river behind the town ran for the first time in months. There had been a tremendous thunderstorm the night before, and from the echoing heavens the waters had descended. And next morning, excited, we stopped whatever we usually did in the morning, and all went to see the river run. It hastened along, a deep, turbulent, discoloured body of water. But the surprise for a New Zealander was a few hours later, when I could have walked across that same river-bed in my felt slippers—*it had all gone!*

Back in the 'twenties and 'thirties, in a period of severe drought, scurvy had attacked the people—and more and more threaded their way to Hermannsburg. Cattle died in their hundreds, and the Mission people were hard put to it to provide meat and cereals, and the little cemetery filled up. Pastor Albrecht saw with painful reality, that there was no future for them if they had to depend on the brackish wells, and what water they could carry on camel-back. So he got some good friends busy, and three thousand pounds was found, and a pipe-line laid. Now the people have water, and vegetable gardens can be made at the Mission.

That first night, after darkness had fallen—bringing with it a merciful coolness—the people gathered to give us a sing-song under the great moon. It was all most impressive. The singers sat on the sandy ground, though it was only possible to see them in silhouette. We sat on stools. Above, hung the great moon; and I doubt whether I had ever seen it so large. And all about us was space—*we were in the middle of Australia, a thousand miles from the sea!*

When I hush my heart I can hear that singing still. And I can recall the exact moment when the old black song-leader with white-whiskered chin, turned to the pastor

233

for some talk, and then to me, to say, 'The people would now like to hear about the Maoris in New Zealand.'

At first, it seemed a task simple enough; but before I could get on to my feet, I knew that it was going to be quite impossible. What could I say to those people about the Maoris in New Zealand? To those people who had never seen the sea? Every tribal history of the Maoris began with the sea. What could I say to folk who had no flowing rivers? Who did no fishing, no swimming? Who built for themselves no houses, who did no carving? Who had no reeds and rushes for handcrafts? What was there left to tell about the Maoris in New Zealand? I thought to myself, I will tell them about their Churches and schools. I will tell them that they also have 'pastors'. Then I will tell them how they cooked their food in the old days—and do still when they are entertaining in a large way. In imagination, I dug the 'hangi', the huge hole in the earth, into which they put the stones to be heated, and the burning logs to kindle them. And I spun it out. I got the stones glowing, and I put in the green leaves—in imagination—and I sprinkled them with water, and got the steam rising. Then I put in the meats, more green leaves, and the potatoes and sweet corn. And that seemed to be understood.

Then I had a brain-wave. I thought: I'll tell them how they greet their friends. It wasn't their habit, I said, to greet their friends with a handshake as the pastor had greeted me, or even with a kiss as very friendly white people greeted each other. They greeted each other, I said, with a pressing of noses—and if, I added, Pastor Griffiths will stand up, we'll show you how they do it. And I had poor old 'Griff' on his feet before he knew what was going to happen to him—and the whole company roared, they thought it a great joke. And I'll confess it, I was so hard up for anything further to tell them about the

234

Maoris in New Zealand, and it was such a good item, *we did it twice!*

Hermannsburg has a famous old boy in Albert Namatijira—the first aboriginal artist in the world. It was a great privilege to meet Albert. He came in from one of his long camel-trips into the desert an hour before we were due to leave. I had already seen his work. In conversation, I found he spoke English very softly. He acknowledged my interest in his trees and cinnabar rocks. I told him how I had used my ciné camera, to take back with me some record of the strange loveliness of the country he loved so well. Then, greatly daring, I asked him if I might continue to use my camera—asking only that he would take no notice of it whatever. So I got some good shots of Albert.

His was an amazing story of creation. Some fifteen or sixteen years earlier, an Australian artist, Rex Battarbee, had gone up to that great country to paint. Before he left, he had held a two-day exhibition for the Hermannsburg folk. It was, he knew, a daring thing to do, to subject his work to the judgement of those black people.

When he had gone, Albert said to his pastor: 'I also would paint like Mr. Battarbee!' 'All right,' said the pastor, you have a try.' But Albert had only the little dabbly paints and papers of the school-children, and his 'try' wasn't a very good one.

'I think it would be better if you waited,' said the pastor. 'It won't be long. Mr. Battarbee will come again, perhaps in another two years.' Two years must have seemed an eternity to Albert, in which to keep up his enthusiasm, but somehow he managed it. And Mr. Battarbee did come again.

On this second visit he took Albert with him out into the desert as his camel-boy. He gave him some proper materials, he told him one or two general rules—about colour values, perspective and composition—but not enough, of course, to make him a British painter.

The amazing result was—as Mr. Battarbee took pleasure in revealing—that at the end of weeks, Albert's work was fit for exhibition in any of the great galleries. He didn't exhibit it then, but after a time he carried down to Adelaide a sketch done at the end of two weeks, and one done after four weeks, and another after two months. And ever since, it has been the accepted thing for Albert's work to be on exhibition and for him to sell fifty to sixty pictures before the last day. I was happy to bring from Hermannsburg an example of Albert's work. When I talked with him he had never seen the sea, he had never seen a city. But life, of course, is enriched by his uncanny gift of showing to us late-comers, his own country, through his own eyes.

I travelled miles with Padre and Mrs. Griffiths, in their patrol truck. Their service to the white settlers had continued steadfastly since bull-dust was a reality, and bitumen roads a fantastic dream. They have one good road now—running straight north to Darwin—otherwise they journey still on bush tracks and across dry river beds. On one such journey we got stuck despite the fact that 'Griff' was counted one of the best drivers—three times we got stuck, once for an hour, once for three hours. If you have ever tried to dig a big patrol truck out of sand, with the temperature over a hundred, you will know what that means! A highly complicated technique, I found was involved. At the end of three hours I said to 'Griff': 'Man, give it up; it isn't worth it. You'll be knocked up after this, give it up.' He was taking me to a great rocky gap famed for its colour, to do some photography. But 'Griff' merely looked up a moment with his wry smile, and said, 'Look, we'll be as right as a bank once we get out of this. If you're in this stuff for three hours, well, you're stuck—but golly, if you're in it for three days, you're bogged. Then you must give up.'

In those immense spaces help is not always to hand. And space can be cruel.

'Griff' told me of a woman in his area who, until their coming, had never seen a white woman to talk with for fifteen years. And she had five children. Now, of course, there was the Flying Doctor service. John Flynn, a missionary of the Presbyterian Church, had seen the coming of the 'plane and the coming of the wireless, and had claimed these things as servants of God for the Inland. He had called in a young technician, and together they contrived a pedal-wireless. It took years to perfect it, but they persevered until the 'dumb Inland was made to speak, and the deaf distances to hear.' So wonderful was the coming of the doctor, that one old bush-man thought of him almost as a miracle worker. Said he: 'He can put a bandage round the earth in forty minutes.'

The largest cattle-station in the world I found was in these parts—*nine-and-a-quarter million acres!*

In Alice Springs itself, the most imposing building I saw was 'Griffiths House'—part of a dream of those good folk whose name it bears—put up by a grateful Church. It stands to serve boys and girls from far distance parts. At the beginning of the school year they come down and live in the hostel—and go to school and Sunday-school and church—till the year's end. But for this opportunity, they would get little education of any sort. Fifty of them were there when I visited the 'House'—and of that number, not a single one of them had come *a distance under a thousand miles!* Indeed, four little boys who took my fancy especially, had each come fourteen hundred miles!

On the Sunday I led worship in the little church, and I

237

addressed the Sunday-school. I found it splendidly staffed and graded. I had forgotten for the moment the fifty boys and girls of the 'House'—which number in any Sunday-school would provide a steady foundation—fifty boys and girls always on time, fifty boys and girls with lessons prepared, fifty boys and girls with no parents to take them off to the beach during school-time, or to do any other of the silly things that parents do!

When the children were dismissed, 'Griff' said to me: 'You won't realize that the next Methodist Sunday-school from here is eight hundred miles up that way, and eight-hundred and fifty miles down that way! If you took our little Sunday-school and put it down in the centre of your country, you wouldn't have another one in the whole of the country! Which gives one a sense of geography!

XXX

I can still hear Rene's exclamation when on our first journey, we stepped ashore in Australia: 'Why, this is geography!' Then with a twinkle, she added, 'But it's green. It was always red in our geography book at school!'

That, of course, is just one of the surprises of geography. I was with her when she discovered that Holland was not yellow, or Germany mauve, or England pinky-red, like a huntsman's jacket.

I have learned that *one must not take one's own little piece of geography too seriously*. I do not mean that one should not love one's own country best; one can hardly help doing that; but that one should see it *in relationship to the other countries of the world*.

Sometimes, of course, an over-serious love of one's own country can be very charming. Alistair MacLean tells of 'John of the Cattle.' 'He was of Mull. A soft-spoken kind of man. Quick of pride. A treasure-chest of ancient wisdoms and songs and tales. And to speak sooth, as tender a creature as you would meet in with between the dawn and the dark feather of the dusk. But as shrewd as he was kind, and as just as he was both—which is the open secret of the prospering man. . . .

'These islands,' he breathed, with a gesture towards the North, 'Aye, 'tis myself that is as fond of them as a mother of her baby-child, and mind, they are the great favourites with the Good One as well.'

'Indeed,' said I.

'Yes,' he went on, 'or rather, as I should say, *the greatest favourite of all*. Now,' he raised his forefinger impressively,

239

'listen to what I am telling you. The Good One made the Hebrides on the eighth day.'

'The eighth day!' I cried, 'but the Bible. . . .' He waved his hand for silence. 'The Bible is a grand book entirely, and the stories in it are warming to the heart. But, mark you, lad, a man who writes a large book cannot mind everything, and'—he hummed a little at this point—'and like enough the decent man forgot about the Islands being made on the eighth day. But they were, and this was the way of it.

'The world was finished and the Good One was mighty tired and took a rest, and, while He was resting, He thought, "Well, I have let my earth children see the power of my mind, in rock and mountain and flower. And I have shown them the love of my mind, for I have made them happy. But halt," says the Good One to Himself, "I have not shown them the beauty of my mind."

'So the next day, and that was the eighth day, He takes up a handful of jewels and opens a window in the sky and throws them into the sea. And those jewels are the Hebrides. (I had the story of it from my father's father,' he finished, 'an extra fine man, and terrible strong for the truth).'

Delightful!

In Millport lived an old parish minister possessed of the same restricted pride. Every Sunday morning, as he led the worship, he prayed: 'God bless the islands of the Greater and Lesser Cumbrae, and the *adjacent islands of Great Britain and Ireland.*'

But there are some aspects of this intense love of one's own geography, that are not so charming. I have heard some of my own countrymen speak of it as 'God's Own Country'. One would have thought that the great world events of the last years would have shown them that there can be no best—that all the little yellow, mauve and pink bits belong together. What touches one touches all; the poverty of one is the poverty of all; the fortune of one is the fortune of all.

There can be no undergirding of our programmes for peace, I believe, until we know this—until those of us who hold the Christian Gospel, interpret it *in the most practical way as a world-gospel.* We need to hear again—in a social, national and international sense—our Lord's words: 'Go ye into all the world and preach the gospel to every creature.' We need to realize more deeply than yet we have done, that this world doesn't belong to Stalin, or to Truman, or Attlee: it belongs to God. And you and I— and all men and women—belong to God.

A little while ago a retiring headmistress was asked what two subjects she would teach if she were beginning again; and she answered without a moment's hesitation: 'Geography—and Obedience!'

In that everlasting commission of our Lord I see them both—the Geography, His; the Obedience, ours!

I lead worship sometimes in a lovely church, where above the communion-table is a chaste cross. And on the communion-table stands a globe—a globe with the angry continents and islands on it; with the lovely Hebrides, the Greater and Lesser Cumbrae, and the little land that is my home. Everyone is accustomed to a globe in the school-room where young minds come to learn, but it has to-day, I believe, even greater significance where men and women come to worship. Once let us bow our heads in sight of that Cross, and in sight of the whole world, and our sense of geography must become greater, our prayer wider, and our serving, and our giving more generous.

XXXI

MANY sunrises have been given since I returned from my journeys; many more since the first chapters of this book were written, but 'the splendour of the sunrise is still upon the circlet of the hills'.

It is not easy to gather up into one final chapter the thoughts that come clamouring for an entrance, for Life is not lived in convenient little chapters; though the purpose and pattern become more and more clear as one goes along.

In dreaming youth I wanted to be an artist, then a teacher, an author, a missionary, a traveller—and in the goodness of God, I have been allowed to weave all these into the pattern of vocation.

None of these belongs tidily to the past, their triumphs and failures, the lessons they have taught me, the disciplines they have imposed, have all spilled over into the present, and become part of personality. Above all, is my gratitude for Life—especially for friends and books, and for the enrichment of mind and spirit which has come to me through the Church to which I belong, and through continual service to other branches of the Christian Church within the world family. One reason why I must finish this book just here, is that before many more sunrises are given, I must leave for England, to attend the Methodist Ecumenical Conference at Oxford. To work and worship with other members of the Christian world family is to me the highest privilege of Life.

What I owe to travel I have already acknowledged, but something more remains to be said of the friendship I have enjoyed with the many, and with the one in particular. To mention names would be to give this chapter the semblance of a telephone directory; my friends are in many countries.

One of them, I know, feels that the chief reason for writing this book might well be as a tribute to that particular friendship which has been the precious gift of all the years. 'I feel,' says she, 'that you and Rene have made something very wonderful out of your friendship. It really is an accomplishment, you know. You are so different—so nice, and different—yet each so much herself. That's one of the things I think so wonderful about your friendship. And another is that you are so out-reaching toward the rest of us. That is where so many—especially women—come to grief. They tend to live in each other's pockets, to turn in upon themselves—and their friendships shrivel up in exclusiveness, or die in one great moment of jealousy or distrust. They don't seem to realize that respect for each other's differences, each other's right to be a person, and to hold an opinion, is the very beginning of it.

'You must have taught each other a tremendous lot through the years; and of course, you've had the fun of knowing each other's friends, and because you haven't conformed to a pattern, you've kept each other fresh. I think it's quite wonderful—so that when I come into your home, I feel that there is a healthy wind blowing. And I go away just a few inches taller, stronger and more purposeful.

'Vera Brittain's *Testament of Friendship* has been said to be the first contribution of its kind to our literature; but your friendship over these twenty packed years, seems to me as grand—grand because it's so jolly normal, and rich and happy. If only you could get it down in writing, but then, perhaps it's hard to do that. I am sure its secret lies somewhere within the phrase you once coined for me when we spoke about it, "we are bonded together in a sweet liberty".'

B——, my friend, is right; it is not easy to set down these things. And for the present, I shall content myself with copying here George Eliot's words, which are full of a lovely significance: 'Those children of God to whom it has been granted to see each other face to face, and to hold communion together, and to feel the same spirit working in both, can never more be sundered, though the hills may lie between. For their souls are enlarged for evermore by that union, and they bear one another about in their thoughts continually, as it were a new strength.'

What more of life than this
  May any one desire—
A sheaf of corn, a kiss,
  A song, a winter fire,
A friend of little speech,
  A gospel-page to turn,
A little good to teach,
  A little good to learn.

                    —JOHN DRINKWATER.